BASIC TERMINOLOGY FOR THERAPEUTIC RECREATION AND OTHER ACTION THERAPIES

SCOUT LEE GUNN, Ed. D.
University of Illinois

Fourth Corrected Printing

Copyright 1975
STIPES PUBLISHING COMPANY

ISBN 0-87563-094-4

Published by
STIPES PUBLISHING COMPANY
10 - 12 Chester Street
Champaign, Illinois 61820

To my students,

human beings for all seasons.

BASIC TERMINOLOGY FOR THERAPEUTIC RECREATION

AND OTHER ACTION THERAPIES

TABLE OF CONTENTS

It has taken a number of years and many experiences to be able to identify and compile what I feel to be the most basic terminology used in settings where therapeutic recreators work, and I firmly believe that understanding and being able to relate to this basic language is the foundation for job effectiveness. Hopefully my sharing this material with others will simplify the process of becoming a competent professional in therapeutic recreation and other action therapies.

Several of my friends and colleagues have contributed to the writing of this book. Special thanks go to Dr. Sam Talmadge for introducing me to therapeutic recreation. Much of the materials in this book are a result of endless probing and discussions with practitioners who took the time to help me brainstorm. Additional gratitude is in order for all of my professional friends who reviewed and helped me refine this manuscript. Thanks go to Dr. George Patrick who contributed to the writing of chapter two. Finally, a special note of thanks to my friends, "Dutch" Slade, M.D., Betty Connell, R.N., and Marianna Trekell, Ph.D., for not only their contributions to the writing of this text but also their continuing support.

To my colleagues at the University of Illinois go my thanks and appreciation for their patience and assistance.

Scout Gunn

PREFACE

Therapeutic recreation is a relatively young field still in the early stages of developing its own body of knowledge. Because therapeutic recreation encompasses not only the broad concepts of leisure but also draws from sociology, psychology, social work, medicine, and physical education, it has been necessary for students to take courses sometimes only peripherally related to recreation and therapy. They have also had to laboriously forage through volumes of related works to pick out specific materials related to their needs and interests. My own professional experience, both as a clinician and educator, has cultivated in me a deep sensitivity for relevancy and simplicity.

When I first began working as a therapeutic recreator, I was hindered in my ability to relate to the language used by other professionals with whom I worked. I would hope that this material would help others to avoid like experiences.

INTRODUCTION

Several years ago I saw a poster which read: "Beetles can't talk to butterflies." These words have become a central focus in my entire approach to therapy and education. Undoubtedly some of the most common themes in my classroom focus on "effective communication," "speaking the same language," and "getting where clients are." Therapeutic recreation and some of the other action-oriented therapies have long purported to offer purposeful, treatment-oriented, and therapeutic activities designed to support rehabilitation. Activity therapies have often worked with various professionals from medicine, psychiatry, psychology, social work, and others. However, too often students find their way into various jobs in treatment facilities unarmed with even the most basic medical and psychiatric vocabulary, only to discover that the "beetle position" is most uncomfortable in a room filled with "butterflies." If we in therapeutic recreation are to hold our own on treatment teams and in rehabilitation settings, we must both understand and "speak the language." It is hoped that this type of basic terminology book will give the therapeutic recreator the essential language to communicate skillfully with peers in health and allied health fields.

Chapter I
GENERAL TERMINOLOGY

AAHPER: American Alliance for Health, Physical Education, and Recreation; in 1952 AAHPER organized a Recreation Therapy Section.

A.D.L.: Activities of daily living; any activity done during a day's time, for the purpose of fulfilling daily needs (eating, dressing, etc.).

Active Activities: Those activities entailing more than the usual physical motion, and action required to walk, sit, etc. (e.g., running, jumping, throwing).

Activity Therapy: Activities are used in the treatment of disease or disability. When recreation is classified as an activity therapy, it is used as a means of realizing various treatment goals and not an end in itself; a generic term used in some settings to identify action therapies such as occupational therapy, therapeutic recreation, dance therapy, art therapy, music therapy, etc.

Adapted Activities: Those recreation events which have been adjusted to fit the needs, interests and capabilities of the physically and/or mentally handicapped, including game rules, facilities, equipment, etc.

Adaptive Behavior: The effectiveness or degree with which the individual meets the standards of personal independence and social responsibility expected of his age and cultural group, including (1) maturation, (2) learning, and (3) social adjustment.

Adapted Physical Education: Modified physical activity provided in educational settings to meet the needs of atypical students with physical or psychological disability; the modification of activity is based on medical diagnosis, prescription, and supervision. Developmental activities, games, sports, and rhythms, suited to the interest, capacities, and limitations of students with disabilities who may not successfully engage in unrestricted activities of the general physical education program.

Adapted Recreation: Modified recreational activities provided both in treatment and community settings, facilitating participation in recreational activities on the part of disabled individuals. The modification of the recreational activity is usually based on medical diagnosis, prescription, and supervision. Activities are adapted individually to meet each person's needs.

Adjunctive Therapy: A term implying supplemental treatment. There are several departments in hospitals that are termed adjunctive therapy departments and they function in a supplementary way to aid the principal treatment of the patient. In some hospitals, the Recreation Department is classified as an Adjunctive Therapy--along with Occupation Therapy and Physical Therapy.

Adjustment: The process of establishing a satisfactory relationship between personal needs and desires and the requirements of the physical and social environment.

Affect: A person's emotional feeling tone. "Affect" and "emotion" are commonly used interchangeably.

Anomaly: That which is abnormal; a deviation from the normal standards.

Aquatics Therapy: The utilization of swimming and other water skills in the rehabilitation process of the disabled. Swimming can be adapted to the needs and capabilities of almost every type of disabled person.

A.R.S.: American Recreation Society. In 1949 organized the first group of professional hospital recreators (Hospital Recreation Section of A.R.S.).

Art Therapy: Art is used as a form of treatment, providing the opportunity for healthy self-expression and growth, self-awareness, communication, and skill development. It allows for creativity and freedom of expression.

B.E.H.: Bureau of Education for the Handicapped; a special section under the Health, Education, and Welfare (H.E.W.) Department of the Federal Government.

Behavioral Modification: A therapeutic modality which purports that the environmental conditions under which a person lives determines the majority of his behavior. To the behaviorist, behavior is learned, and appropriate behavior is that which is successful in solving problems in the person's environment. Therefore, behavior can be changed by reinforcing appropriate or successful behavior and punishing unsuccessful or inappropriate behavior, precisely planned, systematic methods of altering observable behaviors. Key concepts include:

1. operant behavior - behavior controlled by its consequences;

2. respondent behavior - reflex behavior controlled by its antecedents;

3. positive reinforcer - stimulus presented as a consequence of a response intended to maintain the response--a reward;

4. negative reinforcer - aversive stimulus, which, if removed as a consequence of a response, increases or maintains the response;

5. contingency - relationship between a given response and its environmental consequences;

6. differential reinforcement - reinforcement of a response under one stimulus condition but not under other stimulus conditions;

7. schedule of reinforcement - pattern for presentation of reinforcers; may be time (fixed or variable intervals) or number (fixed or variable ratio);

8. shaping - development of new behaviors through systematic plan of reinforcement;

9. time out - a period of time in which individual is removed or denied from receiving reinforcers.

Behavior Disorder: A term used to refer to observable general behavioral abnormalities; impaired development of internalized controls, so that the individual cannot effectively cope with the natural and social demands of his environment.

Behaviorism: A body of psychologic theory developed by John B. Watson (1878-1958), concerned chiefly with objectively observable, tangible, and measurable data, rather than with subjective phenomena such as ideas and emotions.

✓ Behavior Therapy: Any treatment approach designed to modify the patient's behavior directly rather than inquiring into the dynamic causation. Typically, the psychopathology is conceptualized as maladaptive behavior. The treatment techniques are adapted from laboratory investigations of learning and may use principles of classical, instrumental, and traumatic avoidance conditioning, reciprocal inhibition and desensitization, simple extinction, etc.

Biblio-Therapy: The guided use of reading to promote healing and recovery.

Body Image: The concept that each person has of his own body as an object in space, independent of and apart from all other objects, including one's attitudes, perceptions, and feelings toward his body and its parts.

Brain Damaged: A brain injury or neurological impairment. An injury to the brain due to such things as a physical blow, pressure, hormonal malfunction, chemical poisoning, or oxygen deficiency.

✓ Catchment Area: In psychiatry, a term borrowed from the English to delineate geographic area for which a mental health facility has responsibility.

Census: The official enumeration of people in a specific place or section. Area census is the official enumeration of patients in a section of the hospital or agency on any given day.

Cerebral: Pertaining to the brain.

Cerebral Palsied: A disability due to damage of centers of the brain before or during birth resulting in imperfect control of the muscles and marked especially by muscular incoordination, spastic paralysis, and speech disturbances. It is estimated that more than half of the cerebral palsied are mentally handicapped. The afflicted is left with deficits in motor control, coordination, balance, speech, hearing or perception. (See extended definition in Chapter PHYSICAL DISABILITIES.)

Change Agent: In therapeutic recreation, the recreation therapist who serves as the catalyst for the positive change or rehabilitation of patients.

Chronic: Long, drawn out: applied to a disease that is not acute. The symptoms are usually slowly progressive.

Client: A person who is ill, handicapped, developmentally disabled, or mentally retarded and who needs some form of specialized or generic service related to his mental or physical impairment. The terms patient, disabled person, handicapped, or resident are sometimes used in place of "client."

Communication Therapy: Teaching or using various communication skills, e.g., touching, talking, gestures, etc., to bring about positive change in one's ability to relate to others.

Comprehensive Health Program: A program of total health care, including health services services and insurance for the agency's employees and their immediate families.

Comprehensive Mental Health Planning: A plan to include all phases of mental health care such as in-patient, out-patient emergency, partial hospitalization, and consultation and education for both children and adults within a given locale.

Consciousness-Raising Groups: Sensitivity rap groups dealing with societal problems common to the members of the group (e.g., "Women's Rights," "Equal Rights," etc.).

Contracture: A shortening, shrinking or reduction in size of a muscle or group of muscles which may be caused from spasm, paralysis, disuse or maintaining one position for a prolonged period of time.

Convalescent: A person recovering from an illness or surgical operation. A patient who is in the stage of recovery.

Corrective Therapy: The treatment of patients by medically prescribed physical exercises and activities designed to strengthen and coordinate functions and to prevent muscular decline resulting from lengthy convalescence or inactivity due to illness. It places emphasis on functional training and practice in the more advanced stages of rehabilitation, and makes use of various types of exercises and modified sports activities; approved by the American Corrective Therapy Association.

Craft Therapy: Various forms of crafts used as a form of treatment, providing the opportunity for healthy self-expression and growth, structured experiences, and skill development. Unlike art therapy, craft therapy does not allow for creative self-expression, but for structured productive experiences.

Creative Recreation: Activities which provide opportunity for production, formation, origination, and outlet for man's creative urge. Arts and crafts, dance, drama and music are examples of creative recreation.

Culturally Normative: That which is normal, typical, or usual for a given culture, such as the attitudes, performances or behaviors ordinarily displayed by or expected of most individuals within a given culture.

Dance Therapy: The utilization of the tools of basic dance movement and rhythmic action as a means toward non-verbal communication. It is based on the view that expressed feeling, meaningfully shaped, can aid in the integration of the personality and growth in the ability to relate to others.

Developmental Disabilities: Disabilities that become evident in childhood, are expected to continue indefinitely, constitute a substantial handicap to the affected individual, and are attributable to mental retardation, cerebral palsy, epilepsy, or other neurological conditions requiring treatment.

Diagnosis: The determination and/or identification of the specific disease or condition from the symptoms and history presented.

Diagnostic Group: A collection of individuals having the same diagnosis.

Direct Leadership: Leadership in which the leader works with a group face to face. Oral and physical directions are usually given by a direct leader. Direct leadership generally stresses personal dynamics.

Disabled: Refers to individuals who because of impairments are limited or restricted in executing some skills, performing tasks, or participating in certain activities, movements, or patterns.

Disability: The impairment or defect of a bodily organ or member. Disability usually refers to the sense organs and/or organs of execution such as arms, legs, and tongue, but may also apply to mental impairment. Personal inability to cope with certain aspects of the environment as a result of physical or mental impairment or social barriers.

Disabling Conditions: Include but not limited to: hearing impairments, illness and infirmity, low level physical fitness, specific motor deficiencies, physical underdevelopment, mental retardation (mild, moderate, severe, and profound), neurological impairments and brain damage, physical and orthopedic handicaps, special health problems (cardiac disorders, multiple sclerosis, muscular dystrophy, obesity, malnutrition, diabetes, asthma), serious mental maladjustments, emotional disturbances, and social maladjustments, visual handicaps, and culturally, socially, or economically deprived.

Diversionary Activities: Those pursuits or actions which divert the mind from care, business or study, thus causing relaxation and/or amusement.

Educational Therapy: The utilization of instruction in academic areas of education, consciously used to develop the mental and physical capabilities of hospitalized patients. Discussion groups often serve to promote motivation and social involvement.

EKG: Electrocardiogram; the recorded electrical impulses of the heart, helps in the diagnosis of cases of abnormal cardiac rhythm and myocardial damage.

EEG: Electroencephalogram; a graphic recording of minute electrical impulses arising from activity of cells in the brain. Used in neurologic and psychiatric diagnosis and research.

Etiology: Causation, particularly with reference to disease.

Family Therapy: Treatment of more than one member of the family simultaneously in the same session. The treatment may be supportive, directive, or interpretive. The assumption is that a mental disorder in one member of a family may be a manifestation of disorder in other members and in the interrelationships and functioning as a total group.

Generic Services: Services offered or available to the general public, as distinguished from specialized services that are intended only for the disabled.

Gestalt Psychology: A German school of psychology that emphasizes a total perceptual configuration and the interrelations of its component parts.

Gestalt Therapy: In contrast to psychoanalysis, Gestalt therapy emphasizes the here and now, with the awareness of experience and varying behaviors. The general processes include: living in the present, awareness, and responsibility. The usual, a status quo, involves holding on to past behavior and roles, or attempting to obtain environment support by manipulation rather than utilizing self-support. The Gestalt therapist contends that only by directly experiencing feelings (e.g., boredom, fear, pain) in the present can one find what he attempts to avoid and begin to utilize more self-potential. The basic principles of Gestalt therapy are largely the work of Frederick S. Perls.

Graffiti Therapy: The utilization of a graffiti board to promote interaction, communication, and self-expression on the part of patients.

Group: Two or more people between whom there is an established pattern of psychological interaction; it is recognized as an entity, by its own members and usually by others, because of its particular type of collective behavior.

Group Activity: A recreation pursuit carried on by a collection of individuals. Group activities are designed to meet the social needs and interests of the group and stimulate socialization.

Group Dynamics: The complex forces (such as desire for good will, recognition) that are acting upon every group throughout its existence which cause it to behave the way it does. This term is also used to describe a field of study--a branch of the social sciences concerned with using scientific methods to determine why groups behave as they do.

Group Process: A general term for the way a group goes about solving a common problem.

Group Therapy: Treatment of psycho-social problems using interacting forces in small group settings (6-12 persons), requiring a trained leader.

Group Work: Recreational, social, educational, and cultural activities in the community to further the satisfactions and growth of participating group members by providing positive experiences through the group activity programs, interaction with other group members, and interaction of the group with the community. The trained group worker is skilled and knowledgeable in individual and group behavior and community relations. Also called "social group work."

Habilitation: Process of establishing or bringing into existence functional behaviors as related to basic growth and development.

Halfway House: A specialized facility designed to provide a bridge between a residential facility and the community. For clients who do not require full hospitalization or institutionalization but who need an intermediate degree of protection and support before returning to fully independent community living.

Handicapped: Refers to individuals who because of impairments or disabilities are adversely affected psychologically, emotionally, or socially; reflects an attitude of self-pity, feeling sorry for one's self, and despair. One may have a severe impairment or disability and not consider himself/herself to be "handicapped."

Health: The state of optimum capacity of an individual for the effective performance of the roles and tasks for which he has been socialized.

Holistic: In psychiatry, an approach to the study of the individual as a unique entity, rather than as an aggregate of physiological, psychological, and social characteristics.

Homebound: Those persons confined to their residences due to illness or disability.

Hospital Community: See Chapter GENERAL MEDICAL TERMINOLOGY.

Hospital Recreator: See Chapter GENERAL MEDICAL TERMINOLOGY.

House Parent: An individual employed to provide supervision and guidance to children, adolescents, and/or adults as a surrogate mother or father in a residential setting.

Hydrotherapy: The use of water in the treatment process.

Ill: A state contrary to good health. A very nebulous term which is conceived of differently in various cultures.

Ill and Handicapped: A collective term that includes all classifications of persons who are suffering from disease or are disabled.

Impaired: Refers to individuals who have identifiable organic and/or functional conditions --some part of the body is missing, a portion of an anatomical structure is gone, or one or more parts of the body do not function properly or adequately. The condition may be permanent as in amputations, or temporary as in learning disabilities or emotional problems.

Indirect Leadership: Leadership in which the influence of the leader over the follower is transmitted by other people and/or thoughts and suggestions. Face-to-face procedure is not necessary in indirect leadership.

Individual Activity: A recreation pursuit that can be carried on by one person. Examples of individual activities are jigsaw puzzles, solitaire, and weaving. Individual activity and individual recreation are used here as synonyms.

Individualized Prescriptive Recreation Programs: The studying, analyzing, adapting and planning of recreation activities to meet the different abilities, interests and needs of individual clients.

Industrial Therapy: The therapeutic use of activities related to the operation of the hospital (or other therapeutically used facilities) including involvement on the part of the patients in working capacities such as: carpenter, kitchen worker, electrician, plumber, etc. It provides a natural work setting in which to observe the progress, capabilities, etc. of the patient.

In-Patient: One whose treatment necessitates his residence in a hospital for a period of time.

In-Service Training: A training program occurring after appointment and during employment designed to make leaders more effective in their work and aware of the changes occurring in the field of recreation. It is provided primarily by the employing agency and is a continuous program for all workers in the department --professional and volunteer. Some of the methods used to accomplish in-service training are institutes, workshops, staff meetings, trips, demonstrations, and conferences.

Institution: An organization of public, or semi-public nature, involving a directive body and a physical establishment of some sort. It is designated to serve some recognized and authorized end. Hospitals are examples of institutions.

Institutional Recreation: Activities provided by an establishment for its patients, inmates and/or staff.

Interdisciplinary Approach: An approach to diagnosis, evaluation, and individual program planning in which professional and other personnel participate as a team. Each participant, utilizing whatever skills, competencies, insights, and perspectives his particular training and experience provide, focuses on identifying the developmental needs of the person and devising ways to meet them, without constraints imposed by assigning particular domains of behavior or development to particular disciplines only. Participants share all information and recommenddations, so that a unified and integrated habilitation program plan is devised by the team. The interdisciplinary approach is contrasted with the multi-disciplinary approach, in which each representative of a particular discipline or program views the person only from the perspective assigned to his discipline or program; in which particular domains of individual development and behavior are often held to be the sole responsibility or prerequisite of particular professions or programs; and in which each representative of a discipline separately reports his findings and the recommendations that he proposes to implement as a result, more or less independently, of the findings and recommendations reported by other representatives. A single staff member may then use this accumulated knowledge to formulate a program plan.

JOPER: JOURNAL OF PHYSICAL EDUCATION AND RECREATION: the official publication of AAHPER.

Leisure Counseling: A process utilizing verbal facilitation techniques to promote self-awareness, awareness of leisure attitudes, values, and feelings, and the development of decision-making and problem-solving skills related to leisure participation.

Leisure Education: A planned developmental process through which an individual develops an understanding of self and self in leisure, enabling the individual to enhance the quality of life.

Malingering: Deliberate simulation or exaggeration of an illness or disability that, in fact, is nonexistent or minor, in order to avoid an unpleasant situation or to obtain some type of personal gain.

Mainstreaming: The process of selecting methods of integrating people and programs that are as close to a typical way of doing things as possible; the placement of handicapped individuals into the least restrictive environment possible.

Medical Recreator: See Chapter GENERAL MEDICAL TERMINOLOGY.

Milieu Therapy: Literally, treatment by environment in a hospital setting. Physical surroundings, equipment, and staff attitudes are structured in such a way as to enhance the effectiveness of other therapies and foster the patient's rehabilitation; a cooperative effort on the part of various medical and treatment special specialists in the health fields. See Chapter PSYCHIATRIC DISABILITIES.

MMPI: (Minnesota Multiphasic Personality Inventory) A questionnaire type of psychological test designed for persons sixteen years of age and over. It may be administered individually or in groups. Although the MMPI had certain limitations, as a self-reporting test it is one of the most carefully validated and reliable instruments of its kind.

Multiply Handicapped: See Chapter MENTAL RETARDATION.

Music Therapy: The therapeutic use of music as a medium through which patients may be reached and involved, and in which they may find emotional expression and release, skill development, and a sense of self worth. Approved by the National Association for Music Therapy.

NART: National Association of Recreation Therapists; organized in 1952; the official publication was "Recreation for the Ill and Handicapped." In 1965 the NART merged into the National Park and Recreation Society.

Non-Directive Counseling: A "client-centered" Rogerian based technique utilizing "reflective listening" to help the client explore the true nature of their problem. Both verbal and non-verbal messages are reflected back to the client by the counselor. The counselor assumes no responsibility for solving the problems of clients. He assumes a totally accepting, objective position with the client in an effort to help solve his own problems, through exploration, understanding, and self-initiated action. Non-directive therapy concentrates upon empathy, warmth, and unconditionally elicits self-exploration during the exploratory relationship.

Non-Directive Play: Activities engaged in by a person without progressive regulations or rules formulated by another. Non-directive play is frequently employed in pediatric hospital and psychiatric settings.

Normal: That which is usual, expected, understood in its frame of reference, and generally regarded as desirable.

Normalization: The process of providing for a typical rhythm of life for the handicapped; mainstreaming.

NRA: See Chapter PHYSICAL DISABILITIES.

NRPA: National Recreation and Park Association, the major national professional recreation organization.

NTRS: National Therapeutic Recreation Society, the national professional organization for recreation therapists.

NWAA: See Chapter PHYSICAL DISABILITIES.

NWBA: See Chapter PHYSICAL DISABILITIES.

Objectives: A frame of reference that provides measuring rods for use in reaching goals. Objectives may be for one event, a program within a specific setting, or the expression of the philosophy of the recreation profession.

Occupational Therapy: A therapy that utilizes purposeful activities as a means of altering the course of illness, and increasing independent living. The patient's relationship to staff personnel and to other patients in the occupational therapy setting is considered to be therapeutic, and is emphasized in treatment planning. Included are teaching skills of specific trades, arts, and domestic activities as a means for the rehabilitation of physically or mentally handicapped patients.

Out-Patient: A patient who goes to the hospital, clinic or dispensary for diagnosis and/or treatment, but does not occupy a bed overnight.

Paralympics: See Chapter PHYSICAL DISABILITIES.

Participation: Entry into and/or identification with a recreation activity. Participation may be active, passive, or secondary.

Passive Activities: Those activities requiring less than normal physical participation. Passive activities are usually of a spectator nature.

Patient: A person receiving treatment under the care of a physician.

Patient Recreation Council: An elected or appointed group of patients representing build-
ings, wards, floors, or other geographical areas of an institution. The expressed purpose of the council is to advise and plan, with the recreator, the activities
to be included in the recreation program.

Personal Adjustment Training: See Chapter MENTAL RETARDATION.

Physical Therapy: The treatment of disease and injury by physical means, such as light,
heat, cold, water, massage, electricity and exercise. Physical therapy is performed by trained personnel under the prescription of a physician.

Physiotherapy: Treatment of a disease by the physical properties of heat, light, water,
or other mechanical means.

PBO: Planning by Objectives; a system of program planning which utilizes purposes,
goals, and objectives as the primary planning criteria.

Play Therapist: The person, usually on a clinical team, who is responsible for the
children during play periods and at mealtimes but is not involved in nursing
functions. Often helps prepare children for medical procedures or surgery
through such activities as dramatic play or earnest and factual conversation.
May use a psychotherapeutic approach to a child's emotional problems, using
observation and interpretation of play as part of the therapy process.

Play Therapy: A psychotherapeutic approach to children's emotional problems in which
the observation and interpretation of the child's use of his play materials and
his fantasy in his games/play form part of the therapy.

Policy: Directives, rules or regulations concerning management or procedures.
Policies provide guidelines in order to effect the purposes as may be unique to
a particular institution.

Prescribed Recreation: Activities prescribed by a physician. Prescribed recreation may
take the form of a specific activity, or the recreation setting where free choice
of activity is allowed.

Prescription: The act of prescribing or directing the administration of a remedy. A
prescription for recreation usually includes basic information about the patient,
his diagnosis, and limitations. A recreation prescription does not necessarily,
eliminate free choice of activity, but it may do so. The prescription may be
written and signed by a doctor or may be given orally by a doctor.

Professional Recordings: A written report about a patient, a group of patients, or an activity, as observed by the professional recreator. The recording may become
part of the recreation files and/or medical records and is used as a tool of
evaluation.

Prognosis: A prediction of the duration, course and termination of a disease, based on
all information in the individual case and knowledge of how the disease generally
behaves.

Psychodrama: An extemporaneous dramatization performed by the patients, designed to
afford catharsis and social relearning for one or more of the participants from
whose life situation the plot is abstracted; used by psychologists, psychiatrists,
social workers, and activity therapists in the treatment of mental disorders.

Psychotherapy: The treatment of mental or emotional disorders or of related bodily ills by psychological means; counseling, group therapy, etc.

Rapport: A harmonious relationship between two or more people, thereby giving rise to communication. The term implies the persons are capable of responding easily and with apparent spontaneity to each other.

Reality Orientation: See Chapter GERONTOLOGY.

Reality Therapy: A systematic approach to therapy that leads the patient toward reality, toward coping successfully with the tangible and intangible aspects of the real world; emphasis is on the psychiatric version of the R's: reality, responsibility, and right and wrong; an approach to psychiatry developed by William Glasser, M.D.

Recreation Therapy: Recreational activities are used as a form of treatment to assist in the overall rehabilitation of the patient. Recreation as a therapy is used as a means of achieving established treatment goals concomitant with the overall treatment plan for the client. The recreational experience is not an end in itself, but rather a means of achieving an end.

Referral: The act of directing a person to another person, department or agency for assistance. The term may also mean the person being referred to another person or place.

Reflective Listening: A systematic technique (developed by Carkhuff) of "hearing" all of the messages sent by an individual and reflecting back to him accurately his thoughts, expressions, and underlying feelings; a non-directive, Rogerian approach to counseling.

Rehabilitation: To restore, to rebuild, to return to as near normal as possible. The process of restoring a pateint to satisfactory physical, mental, vocational, or social status after injury or illness including mental illness.

Relaxation Therapy: Various techniques in mental and physical relaxation are used as a form of treatment, allowing the patient to better cope with stressful situations while promoting healthful living.

Remedial: Change or improve function or structure by means of selected exercises or activities.

Remission: A lessening or disappearance of the symptoms of a disease; also the period in which this occurs.

Remotivation Therapy: The planned process of reactivating old interests and abilities, in the elderly, depressed, and individuals with acquired disabilities.

Residential Facility: See Chapter GERONTOLOGY.

Rogerian Therapy: A non-directive approach to counseling, utilizing reflective listening (hearing the words, thoughts and feelings of the patient and reflecting them back to the patient accurately to assist him in gaining insight into his problems).

Role Playing: A method of studying the nature of a certain role or problems by acting out a contrived situation; educational technique stressing the "learn through doing" approach.

Service Delivery System: The total array of service components, specialized and generic, that are directed toward meeting the general and particular needs of the disabled.

Severe Handicap: A disability which requires multiple services over an extended period of time and results from amputation, blindness, cancer, cerebral palsy, cystic fibrosis, deafness, heart disease, hemiplegia, mental retardation, mental illness, multiple sclerosis, muscular dystrophy, neurological disorders (including stroke and epilepsy), paraplegia, quadriplegia, and other spinal conditions, renal failure, respiratory or pulmonary dysfunction.

Sheltered Workshop: A workshop for handicapped individuals. The type and tempo of work and machinery are modified for the workers. Payment on a piecework basis provides an income in accordance with the efficiency of the individual.

Short-Term Patient: See Chapter GENERAL MEDICAL TERMINOLOGY.

Short-Term Resident Camp: A creative, cooperative experience in living in the out-of-doors in self-sufficient small groups for periods of five days or less.

Special Interest Groups: Groups that are organized because of some particular recreation interests. The group may be interested in learning a new skill, engaging in a particular activity, or concerning themselves with many new experiences around a common theme.

Special Olympics: Athletic events held annually for mentally retarded children and youth, with all the pageantry and ritual characteristic of the traditional Olympics; sparked by the Kennedy Foundation and initiated in the Chicago Park District in 1968.

Special Physical Education: See Adaptive Physical Education.

Special Populations: Those individuals who due to physical or mental disabilities are not normally served by public and commercial recreation programs; includes the physically ill and handicapped, mentally retarded, mentally ill or disturbed, those with learning disabilities, the aged and delinquent and/or imprisoned individuals (some therapeutic recreators would also include the socially disadvantaged).

Special Recreation: A branch of therapeutic recreation interested in providing recreational experiences in community recreation settings for various special populations. Special recreation advocates the accessibility of recreation as an end itself to special populations. It is not concerned with the total treatment process of the individual and is, therefore, not considered therapy.

Special Recreologist: A specialist in the field of therapeutic recreation who understands both the characteristics and needs of special populations, as well as the total working of municipal and/or outdoor recreational settings, and is able to provide and/or integrate recreational programs for special populations into existing public and/or private recreational settings. Though he is familiar with the characteristics of various special populations, he is not considered to be a therapist but rather a specialist advocating the recreational needs of the disabled, elderly, etc.

Sympathetic Nervous System: That part of the autonomic nervous system that responds to dangerous or threatening situations by preparing the individual physiologically for "fight" or "flight."

√Syndrome: A configuration of symptoms that occur together and that constitute a recognizable condition. Example: Ganser's Syndrome.

T-Groups: Sensitivity training groups; a group of people who meet to learn about themselves, about interpersonal relationships, about group process, and about larger social systems. An important element in the learning is that the group members meet in an unstructured situation and have the task of constructing their own group.

Theme-Centered Therapy: Focusing on a central theme and allowing individuals to express all of their related feelings concerning the theme; used as a form of group and individual treatment and education. Should a member of the group stray in thought, the therapist allows the individual to work through their thoughts before returning to the theme. The emphasis is always in the now and expression remains in the first person; developed by Ruth Cohen.

Therapeutic: This term pertains to the treatment of disease or the art of healing; an agent capable of healing; having medical or healing properties.

Therapeutic Play: The use of play as a means of producing information and/or therapy for the person engaged in the activity.

√ Therapeutic Recreation: A generic term denoting services in the field of recreation with a special emphasis on the needs of the ill or handicapped individual. It may also generally encapsulate those activities designed or adapted for members of special populations by a professional recreator. The activities and the clients participation in them are structured to be therapeutic in addition to providing each individual with an opportunity for the recreation experience. The field of Therapeutic Recreation includes both an emphasis in "Recreation Therapy," "Leisure Education for the Handicapped," and "Special Recreation."

√ Therapeutic Recreator: A recreator with specialized training in growth and development, diaabilities, psychology, sociology, and medicine, and possessing the skills to facilitate the use of activities as a therapeutic tool in the accomplishment of treatment objectives and rehabilitation.

Therapeutics: Branch of science concerned with the application of remedies and the tre ment of disease.

Therapy: The treatment of disease or pathological condition; or a special type of procedure used in the treatment of disease or injury: a synonym for treatment.

Total Push Program: A program designed to use most of the patient's waking day in some type of carefully planned, scheduled therapeutic activity. The patient is encouraged to actively participate in each scheduled activity as well as develop relationships with other patients and staff.

Transactional Analysis (TA): A rational method of analyzing and understanding behavior developed by Eric Berne; purports that all behavior stems from one of three parts to man's personality--the Parent, the Child, or the Adult. The "Parent" is that behavior which we learn from our own parents. The "Child" is the way in which we responded as a child. The "Adult" is the part of us that reasons out situations and responds maturely and appropriately.

Treatment: The management, medical or surgical care of a patient. Any measure designed to ameliorate or cure an abnormal or undesirable condition.

TRJ: THERAPEUTIC RECREATION JOURNAL, official publication of the NTRS.

Vocational Rehabilitation (VR): A program of retraining persons with physical defects, handicaps, and mental disorders for profitable employment.

Vocational Therapy: Job counseling and training for the ill and disabled.

Volunteer: One who enters into, or offers himself for, any service of his own free will. His work is usually parttime and always without monetary remuneration. Individual services may include such acts as serving on boards and committees, teaching activity fundamentals, and stuffing envelopes. Organizations and groups may also render volunteer services.

Weed System: A systematic way of recording a patient's progress by stating chronologically (1) all of the patient's presenting problems, (2) treatment goals for each problem, (3) treatment plan, and (4) regular progress in each problem area; developed as a medical model by Dr. Weed; a method of implementing individualized prescriptive programming.

Wheelchair Sports: See Chapter PHYSICAL DISABILITIES.

Chapter II

AN EASY APPROACH TO UNDERSTANDING MEDICAL TERMINOLOGY

The approach used in this chapter* attempts to give the student and practitioner rudimentary skills in deciphering medical terminology by defining components frequently used in medical words. Common usages, given here, may differ in some instances from original literal meanings. However, the individuals who gain command of these components should be able to identify at a glance a large number of combined terms. This basic basic approach is not a substitute for knowledge of physiology, anatomy, pathology, or medicine. The student should expect this to be the initial step in building a medical vocabulary. Frequent use of these terms relevant to specific disabilities and surrounding implications, both in simulated learning environments and clinical internships, should begin to provide the student with a working knowledge of basic medical terminology. In order to enhance the understanding and to be aware of relationships and uses of terms, additional key words identifying body positions, postures, planes, structures and muscles are also included in this chapter.

PREFIXES

Prefixes	Translation	Examples
a- (an- before a vowel)	without, absence of	apathy, lack of feeling; aphasia, without speech; aplasia, absence of growth
ab-	away from	abduct(-ion), move away from medial line of the body; aboral, away from the mouth
ad-	towards, near to	adduct(-ion), move towards the medial plane; adhesion, to stick to; adrenal, near the kidney
ambi-	both	ambidextrous, ability to use both hands equally; ambilaterality, both sides
ante-	before, in front of, forward	antecubital, before elbow; anterior; anteflexion, forward bending
anti-	opposed to, against	antihistamine, a drug acting in opposition to histamine; antiperistalsis, reversed peristalsis; antisepsis, against infection
bi-	twice, double	bifocal, two foci; bilateral, both sides

---

* Dr. George Patrick assisted in the writing of this chapter.

Prefixes	Translation	Examples
bio-	life	biopsy, visual examination (usually under microscope) of tissues from living subject
cardi-	heart	cardiac
√cata-	down, complete	catatonic, mental disorder characterized by stupor and muscular tension, sometimes extreme emotional outbursts, one type schizophrenia; cataract, lens of eye becomes completely opaque.
circum-	around, about	circumduct, move in a circle; circumcision, removal of foreskin around penis
con-	with, together	congenital, present at birth
contra-	against, opposite	contraindicated, not indicated; contraception, prevention of conception
di-	twice, double	diplopia, double vision; dichromatic, two colors
√dia-	through, across, completely	diaphragm, wall across; diathermy, heat treatment through the muscle tissues by high-frequency electric current; diagnosis, complete knowledge
dis-	separating, apart, reversal	dissect, cut apart; dislocate, joint wrenched out of socket
dys-	bad, difficult, disordered	dysplasia, disordered growth; dyspepsia, bad digestion; dyspnea, difficult breathing
e-, ex-	out, away from	evert, turn outwards; exotosis, boney outgrowth (spur)
√ecto-	outside	ectoderm
ectomy-	excision	tonsillectomy
endo-	within	endoderm
epi-	upon, on	epidural, upon dura (brain or spinal covering); epilepsy, (upon and seize) chronic disease of the nervous system characterized by convulsions or unconsciousness

Prefixes	Translation	Examples
✓ gyn-	female	gynecology, study of diseases of women
hem(o)-	blood	hemopheliac, free bleeder
✓ hemi	half	hemiplegia, paralysis of half of the body (partial paralysis)
hetero-	different	heterogeneity, having dissimilar ingredients
homo-	same	homologous, corresponding in structure
hydro-	fluid, water	hydrocele, collection of fluid esp. along spermatic cord; hydrocephalic, fluid excess in cranium causing enlargement of the head and wasting away of the brain.
hyper-	above, in excess of, normal	hypertrophy, excess growth; hyperactivity; hypertension
hypo-	under, below, deficient	hypodermic, beneath the skin; hypotension
infra-	below	infraclavicular, below the collarbone
intra-	within	intracranial, within the cranium (skull); intraspinal
kine-	movement	kinesiology; kinesthetic, the feel of the movement
mal-	bad	malnourished; malignancy, bad growth (cancer)
men-	month	menopause, cessation of monthly menstruation
micro-	small	microcephalic, having a small head
✓ my(o)-	muscle	myalgia, muscular pain
meta-	beyond, after, change	metastasis, beyond original position; metacarpal, beyond the wrist
para-	beside, sides	paraplegia, paralysis of both sides
per-	through, excessive	permeate, pass through
peri-	around	periapical, around the apex of the tooth; peribronchial, around bronchial area

Prefixes	Translation	Examples
pneumo-	lung	pneumonia, lung infection
post-	after, behind	post-natal, after birth; post-operative, after operation
pre-	before	pre-operative, before surgery
pro-	before, in front of	prognosis, foreknowledge
pseudo-	false	pseudo-angina
psych-	mind	psychogenic, produced in the mind
✓ retro-	behind	retrocervical, located behind the cervix
semi-	half	semilunar cartilage, half-moon cartilage
sub-	below	subnormal
supra-	above	suprascapula, above the scapula
sym-, syn-	with, together	symphysis, growing together; synarthrosis, articulation of joints together
tox-	poison	toxin
trans-	across	translucent
uni-	unilateral, on one side	

SUFFIXES

Suffixes	Use	Examples
✓ -ize, -ate	add to nouns or adjectives to make verbs expressing to use and to act like; to subject to; make nto	visual (able to see); impersonate (act like); hypnotize (put into state of hypnosis)
-ist, -or, -er	add to verbs to make nouns expressing agent or person concerned or instrument	anesthetist (one who practices the science of anesthesia); dissector (instrument that dissects or person who dissects); donor (giver)
-ent	add to verbs to make adjectives or nouns of agency	recipient (one who receives); concurrent (happening at the same time)

Suffixes	Use	Examples
-sia, -y, -tion	add to verbs to make nouns expression action, process or condition	therapy (treatment); inhalation (act of inhaling); anesthesia (process or condition of feeling)
✓ -ia, -ity	add to adjectives of nouns to make nouns expressing quality or condition	septicemia (poisoning of blood); disparity (inequality); acidity (condition of excess acid); neuralgia (pain in nerves)
-logy	study of	psychology, study of the mind
✓ -lysis	breaking up, dissolving	renaldialysis, separation of urine from blood
-tomy	cut, incise	appendectomy, removal of the appendix
-trophy	nourish, grow	atrophy, dystrophy
-ma, -mata, -men, -mine, -ment	add to verbs to make nouns expressing result of action or object of action	trauma (injury); foramina (openings); ligament (tough fibrous band holding bone or viscera together)
-ium, -olus, -olum, -culus, -cule, -cle	add to nouns to make diminutive nouns	bacterium; alveolus (air sac); follicle (little bag); cerebellum (little brain); molecule (little mass); ossicle (little bone)
-ible, -ile	add to verbs to make adjectives expressing ability or capacity	contractile (ability to contract); edible (capable of being eaten); flexible (capable of being bent)
-al, -c, -ious, -tic	add to nouns to make adjectives expressing relationship, concern	neural (referring to nerve); neoplastic (referring to neoplasm); cardiac (referring to heart); delirious (suffering from delirium)
✓ -id	add to verbs or nouns to make adjectives expressing state of condition	flaccid (state of being weak); fluid (state of being fluid or liquid)
✓ -tic	add to a verb to make an adjective showing relationship	caustic (referring to burn); acoustic (referring to sound or hearing)
-oid, -form	add to nouns to make adjectives expressing resemblance	polypoid (resembling polyps); plexiform (resembling a plexus); epidermoid (resembling epidermis)

Suffixes	Use	Examples
-ous	add to nouns to make adjectives expressing material	ferrous (composed of iron); serous (composed of serum); mucinous (composed of mucin)
-uria	urine	albumenuria (albumen in the urine)

GREEK AND LATIN COMPONENTS

Greek and Latin

Components	Meaning	Examples
audi(o)-	hear(ing)	audiometer, hearing measurer
centesis	puncture, perforate	enterocentesis, intestinal puncture
duct	lead	oviduct, uterine or fallopian tube
edem	swell	edema, swelling caused by fluid
ethes	feel	anesthesia, without feeling
flex	bend	dorsiflexion, bend toward the back
fiss	split	fissure
geno, genesis	produce, origin	genotype; pathogenesis, origin of disease
liga	bind	ligament ligation
necro	dead	necrophobia, fear of death
op, opto	see, vision	myopic, nearsighted; amblyopia, partial blindness
oxy	sharp, quick	oxyesthesia, sharpened feelings
par, partus	labor	postpartum, after birth
pep	digest	dyspepsia; peptic ulcer
phas	speak, utter	aphasia, unable to speak
phobia	fear	hydrophobia, fear of water
plas	form, grow	rhinoplasty, nose surgery
proct-	rectum	proctoscopy, examine the rectum
pron (e or us)	face down	prone

Greek and Latin

Components	Meaning	Examples
schiz-	split	schizophrenia, personality split from reality
sclero	hard	arteriosclerosis, hardening of arteries
scolio	twisted, crooked	scoliosis, spinal curvature
steno	narrow	mitral stenosis, narrow valve in heart
supinus	face up	supine

BODY POSITIONS AND DIRECTIONS

There are a number of anatomical terms used in describing the body and determining position and direction. When the arms are hanging to the side, palms facing forward, with the body erect, the following terms are used to describe direction and position:

anterior - toward the front or ventral side of the body

✓ posterior - toward the back or dorsal side of the body

medial - nearer to or toward the midline

lateral - farther from the midline or the side of the body

internal - inside

✓ external - outside

✓ proximal - nearer to the point of origin or closer to the body

distal - away from the point of origin or away from the body

superior - above

✓ inferior - below

cranial - toward the head

✓ caudal - toward the lower end of the body (cauda means tail)

ANATOMICAL PLANES OF THE BODY

Certain anatomical planes are used to identify structures and areas of the body as follows:

The medial (midsagittal) or midline is an imaginary plane that passes from the front to the back through the center of the body and divides the body into right and left equal portions.

The sagittal plane is a section parallel to the long axis of the body or parallel to the median plane and divides the body into right and left unequal parts.

The frontal (coronal) plane is a section through the side of the body, passing at right angles to the median plane and dividing the body into anterior and posterior portions.

The transverse plane is a horizontal plane passing at right angles to both the frontal and median planes and dividing the body into cranial and caudal parts.

ANATOMICAL POSTURES OF THE BODY

The terms used to describe anatomical postures are as follows:

erect - body in a standing position.

supine - body lying flat on the back in a horizontal position.

prone - body lying face and trunk down in a horizontal position.

laterally recumbent - body lying horizontally either on the right or left side.

WORD COMPONENTS REFERRING TO BODY STRUCTURES

Component	Pertaining to
angi-	vessel (blood)
arth-	joints
aur-	ear
cardi-	heart
✓ caud-	tail (or lowest part of spine)
✓ chol-	bile ducts, gall bladder
chondr-	cartilage
col-	colon
dactyl-	finger
derm-	skin

Component	Pertaining to
✓ encephol-	brain
enter-	intestine
fibro-	fibrous connective tissue
gastro-	stomach
gloss-	tongue
hepat-	liver
hyster-	uterus
mamm-, mast-	breast
myel-	bone marrow or spinal cord
myo-	muscle
nephr-	kidney
ocul-	eye
opthalm-	eye
or-	mouth
✓ oste-	bone
ot-	ear
phleb-	vein
pneumo-	lung
proct-	rectum
ren-	kidney
rhin-	nose

BASIC MUSCLES AND RELATED ANATOMICAL TERMS

Antagonist: a muscle acting in opposition to another.

Biceps: refer to a muscle of the upper arm called biceps brachii and a leg muscle called biceps femoris. Biceps refers to the two insertions of the muscle, and brachii means arms.

Brachialis: arm muscle that flexes the forearm.

Deltoid: muscle that clasps the shoulder.

Diaphragm: musculomembranous partition between abdomen and thorax.

Erector spinae: deep muscles of the back that aid in maintaining balance.

Extensors: muscles that extend a part. There are a number of these muscles in the wrists, fingers, ankles and toes. See medical dictionary for proper names.

Fascia: sheath holding muscle fibers or bundles together. The plural is fasciae. The dense fibrous membranes investing the trunk and limbs, with sheaths to various muscles in close proximity, are called deep fasciae.

Flexors: muscles that flex a joint. There are a number of these muscles in the wrist, fingers and foot. See medical dictionary for proper names.

Gastrocnemius: a lower leg (calf) muscle that somewhat resembles the shape of the stomach. Gastro means stomach, and cnemius refers to the leg.

Gluteus: referring to hip; the maximus, medius, and minimus hip muscles that regulate movement of the hip joint.

Gracilis: an inner thigh muscle that adducts the femur and flexes the knee joint.

Iliacus: an ilial muscle that flexes thigh and trunk.

Intercostals: respiratory muscles; muscles situated between the ribs.

Interspinalis: vertebral muscle.

Involuntary muscle: muscle that cannot be moved at will.

Latissimus dorsi: a broad muscle of the back, active in arm movements.

Ligaments: strong bands of tissue that hold bones together and keep organs in place.

Pectoralis major and minor: chest muscles. Pectus refers to the chest or breast.

Popliteus: muscle of the knee.

Quadriceps femoris: a muscle for extending the leg upon the thigh. It has four heads.

Rectus abdominis: a muscle that supports the abdomen and flexes the lumbar vertebrae.

Soleus: a leg muscle that flexes the ankle joint.

<u>Sphincter</u>: muscles that contract or compress, as those of the anus, pupil, urethra.

<u>Tonus</u>: state of tension, present to a degree in muscles at all times.

<u>Trapezius</u>: a superficial muscle of the back of the neck and upper trunk that controls shoulder movements.

<u>Triceps brachii</u>: upper arm muscle.

<u>Voluntary muscle</u>: muscle that can be moved at will.

Chapter III

GENERAL MEDICAL TERMINOLOGY

Abduction: To draw away from midline of the body.

Acute: Sharp, severe; having rapid onset, severe symptoms and a short course; not chronic.

Adduction: To draw toward the midline of the body.

Albino: A person with skin lacking pigmentation resulting in abnormal whiteness of the skin, hair, and eyes.

Alcoholic Deterioration: Permanent damage to the nervous system due to the heavy use of alcohol; characterized by loss of interest and purpose to living; loss of feelings of responsibility, self-deception, untruthfulness, unreliability, difficulty in sexual relations, inability to respond to warmth and affection, and memory failure.

Alcoholic Paranoia: Withdrawal disturbance from heavy use of alcohol characterized by suspiciousness, irritability, jealousy, and hostility.

Ambulatory Patient: The classification given to patients who are not confined to bed. Usually patients in wheelchairs and on crutches are regarded as ambulatory patients.

Amnesia: Inability to remember past experiences; loss of memory.

Angina Pectoris: See Chapter GERONTOLOGY.

Anoxia: Lack of oxygen causing suffocation.

Anterior: Pertaining to the front of a body.

Aphasia: See Chapter GERONTOLOGY.

Arrhythmia: Interrupted rhythm of the heart beat.

Arthritis: A joint condition characterized by inflammation (redness), pain, swelling, and other changes varying with the type, common in the aging process. The general types of arthritis are:

    1. Degenerative: You can think of this as the normal wear and tear upon joints and resulting in some disability and pain as you grow older. Occurs primarily in weight bearing joints, hips, knees.

    2. Rheumatoid: This is an actual disease process with the principal defect lying in the synovium, the fluid that lines and lubricates the joints. Because this is defective, the joints become involved, and swelling, pain, and deformities result. This can affect any joint in the body, is chronic and can begin in youth or during adulthood.

Arthrogryposis: This is a disease of the soft tissue and connective tissue which lies between the muscle cells resulting in multiple congenital contracturss. Muscles
are usually underdeveloped and are replaced by fibrous tissue and fat. The extreme fibrosis affects the joints resulting in the contractures. Most of these
people are able to walk, but have very tight joints and are somewhat skinny.
Again, the degree of involvement varies.

Ataxia: Lack of balance caused by muscular incoordination.

Atrophy: A wasting due to lack of nutrition or use of a part.

Aura: In epilepsy, a premonitory, subjective sensation (e.g., a flash of light) that often
warns the patient of an impending convulsion.

B & B: Bowel and Bladder; organs of elimination (bowel--fecal, and bladder--urine).

Bed Patient: A patient who, because of the nature of his illness, is confined to the bed.

Benign: Not malignant, as in cancer.

CA: Cancer.

Carcinoma: Cancer.

Carcinogenic: Cancer causing.

Cardiac: Pertaining to the heart; a person suffering from a heart condition.

Cardiac Arrest: Heart attack.

Cardiogram: A tracing of the heart rhythms.

Cataracts: Clouding of the lens of the eye or its capsule or both; it can be congenital or
caused by the aging process.

Census: See Chapter GENERAL TERMINOLOGY.

Cerebral: See Chapter GENERAL TERMINOLOGY.

Cerebral Palsied: See Chapter GENERAL TERMINOLOGY.

Chemotherapy: See Chapter PSYCHIATRIC DISABILITIES.

Cirrhosis: Inflammation causing hardening, granulation, contraction of organ tissues;
i.e., cirrhosis of the liver.

COHI-MH: Crippled and other health impaired, multiply handicapped populations; individuals with physiological impairment and concomitant educationally related
problems, requiring some modification of programs to meet their educational
needs; the learning process has been affected by a physical or health impairment or secondary functional disability.

Coma: A state of complete loss of consciousness.

Concussion: Dizziness, nausea, loss of consciousness, weak pulse, and slow respiration
caused by a severe blow to the head.

Congenital: Existing at the time of or before birth.

Contracture: See Chapter GENERAL TERMINOLOGY.

Convulsion: A violent involuntary contraction of voluntary muscles, usually accompanied by loss of consciousness.

Chronic: See Chapter GENERAL TERMINOLOGY.

Convalenscent: See Chapter GENERAL TERMINOLOGY.

✓ CVA: Cerebral Vascular Accident (stroke; caused by the following types of injury to the brain:

    1. Blood clot

    2. Hemorrhage

    3. Compression

    4. Trauma

Decubitus Ulcer: Bed sore, ulceration of the skin and soft tissue, as a result of prolonged pressure. When severe, may penetrate through the muscle to the bone; may develop within 24 hours; especially common to patients lacking tactile sensation; also known as "pressure sores".

Deteriorate: Waste away.

Diagnosis: See Chapter GENERAL TERMINOLOGY.

Disabling Conditions: See Chapter GENERAL TERMINOLOGY.

Distal: Pertaining to the farthest end from the midline.

DOA: Terminology used to indicate that a patient is "Dead on Arrival" at the hospital.

Dorsal: The back of a body.

Dyslexia: Difficulty in reading; confusion of letters "Pot to Top": defect in pathways that connect cerebellum (coordiation) with the inner ear (balance).

Dystrophy: Defective nutrition or development.

Edema: Swelling of a part due to a presence of fluid in the tissue.

EKG: See Chapter GENERAL TERMINOLOGY.

EEG: See Chapter GENERAL TERMINOLOGY.

Embolism: An obstruction of a blood vessel by foreign substance or a blood clot that may move to vital areas of the body and cause immediate death (e.g., to the brain, heart, or lungs); it may be solid, liquid, or gaseous.

Encephalitis: A general term used to delineate a diffuse inflammation of the brain. The condition may be acute or chronic and may be caused by a variety of sgents such as viruses, bacteria, spirochetes, fungi, protozoa, and chemicals (such as lead). In addition to a number of neurological signs and symptoms, a variety of mental and behavioral changes occur during the illness and may persist beyond the acute phase of the illness.

Enuresis: Bed wetting.

Epilepsy: A disorder characterized by periodic motor or sensory seizures or their equivalents, and sometimes accompanied by a loss of consciousness or by certain equivalent manifestations. May be idiopathic (no known organic cause) or symptomatic (due to organic lesions). Usually accompanied by abnormal electrical discharge as shown by EEG.

1. Jacksonian epilepsy: Recurrent episodes of convulsive seizures or spasms localized in a part or region of the body without loss of consciousness. Named after Hughlings Jackson (1835-1911).

2. Major epilepsy (grand mal): Characterized by gross convulsive seizures with loss of consciousness.

3. Minor epilepsy (petit mal): Minor, nonconvulsive epileptic seizures or equivalents; may be limited to only momentary lapses of consciousness.

4. Psychomotor epilespy: Recurrent periodic disturbances, usually of behavior, during which the patient carries out movements often repetitive, highly organized but semi-automatic in character.

Extension: To straighten.

Flaccid: Limp, relaxed, without muscle tone.

Flexion: To bend.

Flexor: Muscle that flexes a joint.

Fracture: To break; as a bone.

Friederich's Ataxia: This is a fairly rare, progressive hereditary nervous disease beginning usually at about 8-12 years of age. It affects the parts of the spinal cord which mediate voluntary control, coordination, and secondly, postural sense and balance. Progression from walking with an unsteady walk to a wheelchair is the usual case. It may appear much like M.S. in the adult. Heart, diabetes and vision problems often occur in conjunction with the basic nervous condition.

Functional: In medicine, changes in the way an organ system operates that are not attributed to known structural alterations. While it is true that psychogenic disorders are functional in that their symptoms are not based on any detectable alterations in the structure of the brain or psyche, it is not true that all functional disorders of the psyche are of emotional origin any more than functional heart murmurs are based on emotional conflict. A drug-induced, temporary disturbance in central synaptic transmission, for example, may produce psychologic or behavioral abnormalities, but such changes in function are not correctly considered to be psychogenic in origin.

FUO: Fever of Unknown Origin.

FX: Fracture.

Gait: Manner or style of walking.

General Hospital: A hospital that accepts for treatment patients with any type of disease.

General Medical Hospital: A hospital that accepts medical patients. Medical hospitals, according to hospital management, includes internal medicine, nervous and mental, tuberculosis, children, communicable disease, and verereal disease services.

General Medical and Surgical Hospital: A hospital that accepts anyone with an illness or injury of physical origin.

Handicapped: See Chapter GENERAL TERMINOLOGY.

Hemophilia: This is a hereditary disease affecting males and impairing the clotting mechanism of the blood. Deep cuts, bruises, too much exercise are very dangerous. A bruise may start bleeding into the joints for a very long time and many of these people have swollen, stiff kness, ankles, elbows because of this permanent tendency to hemorrhage. When the normal person exercises very hard, there are small capillaries that are broken and some minute bleeding into the tissue spaces. In the hemophiliac this bleeding is not checked and stopped. The same goes for a bruise. Usually small superficial cuts will stop, but a deep cut or internal bleeding is very, very serious. Some people will use hot water bottles, fill them with ice and apply this to joints that have recently been bruised to try and stop the bleeding into the joints, and reduce swelling.

Hemiplegia: Paralysis of half of the body (partial paralysis).

Hospital Community: A hospital community includes staff, patients, facilities and services rendered. The community has a common language, interest, recognition and way of life. The hospital community may extend beyond this to include an area served by the hospital.

Hospital Recreator: A term once used to denote a professionally qualified person giving full time to recreation within the hospital setting.

Hyperemia: Excessive blood in any part of the body.

Hypertonic: Abnormally great tension.

Hypertrophy: Abnormally large organ or part of the body, not due to a tumor.

Hyperventilation: Overbreathing associated with anxiety and marked by reduction of blood carbon dioxide, subjective complaints of light headedness, faintness, tingling of the extremities, palpitation, and feelings of inability to get enough air.

Hypotonia: Diminished tension; reduction in muscle tone.

Idiopathic: No known organic cause.

Ill: See Chapter GENERAL TREMINOLOGY.

Ill & Handicapped: See Chapter GENERAL TERMINOLOGY.

Impaired: See Chapter GENERAL TERMINOLOGY.

Incontinence: Loss of control of bladder or bowel or both.

Inferior: Pertaining to the lower part of a body.

In-patient: See Chapter GENERAL TERMINOLOGY.

Intensive Treatment: This term implies that the patient is receiving continuous and extensive treatment, usually in a specifically designated place in the hospital.

Isolation: The limitation of movement and social contacts of a person suffering from an unknown or known carrier of a communicable disease.

Jaundice: Yellow tones to the eyes, skin, urine, and sweat due to presence of bile pigments in the bloodstream.

Kinesthesia: The awareness of muscular motion, weight, and position.

Korsakoff's Psychosis: Gross Vitamin B deficiency in alcoholism, which affects the nervous system and impairs the thought processes; characterized by loss of sense of time and space, memory loss, and false memories of past events.

Lateral: Pertaining to the side.

Legg-Perthes Disease: See Chapter PHYSICAL DISABILITIES.

Long-Term Patient: A person who is ill or disabled over an extended period of time. In terms of national averages for length of stay in hospitals, over eight days may be considered long-term.

Malignant: Growing worse: resistant to treatment. Said of cancerous growths.

Medial: Closest to the midpoint.

Medical Recreator: A term which once denoted a professionally qualified person giving full time service to recreation for in-patients, out-patients, clinic patients and homebound patients. This term differs from Hospital Recreator in that a Medical Recreator does not confine his services to the hospital setting.

Medical Team: A combination of professional medical and para-medical personnel working together to aid in the recovery of the patient.

Metastasis: Movement of bacteria or disease from one part of the body to another.

Mutation: A change in the character of a gene giving rise to new genes.

Necrotic: Dead tissue; death of a portion of tissue.

Neurosurgery: Surgery of the nervous system.

Non-ambulant: A classification given to a patient unable to walk or move about. A bed patient may be referred to a non-ambulant.

Non-ambulatory: Unable to walk independently, without assistance.

Nystagmus: Constant involuntary movement of the eyeball.

Organic Brain Syndrome: See Chapter GERONTOLOGY.

Osteomyelitis: Inflammation of the bone.

Out-Patient: See Chapter GENERAL TERMINOLOGY.

Paramedical Service: A secondary service to medicine. Recreation and social work are examples of paramedical services.

Paraysmpathetic Nervous System: That part of the autonomic nervous system that controls the life-sustaining organs of the body under normal, danger-free conditions.

Pathogenesis: Origination and development of a disease.

Pathogeny: The origin or growth of a disease.

Pathology: Study of the nature and cause of disease which involves changes in structure and function.

Patient: See Chapter GENERAL TERMINOLOGY.

Patient Capacity: The number of patients a hospital can accommodate at one time.

Physical Limitations: The restrictions imposed upon an individual by a temporary or permanent physical disability. An example of temporary physical limitation is surgery. A permanent physical disability example is blindness or deafness. This term may also refer to the physical limitations of a building or facilities.

Posterior: Pertaining to the back of a body.

Post-Hospitalization: This term refers to the time after a patient's discharge from the hospital. The period usually continues until the patient is released from the physician's care.

Prescription: See Chapter GENERAL TERMINOLOGY.

Prognosis: See Chapter GENERAL TERMINOLOGY.

Proprioception: Sensations arising from deeper body tissue such as muscles, ligaments, bones, tendons, and joints.

Pulmonary: Concerning or involving the lungs.

Remission: See Chapter GENERAL TERMINOLOGY.

<u>R.O.M.</u>: Range of Motion; the extent of motion within a given joint. The types of R.O.M. are:

1. <u>Active (R.O.M.)</u>: Motion carried out voluntarily by the patient.

2. <u>Active-Assistive (R.O.M.)</u>: Motion carried out voluntarily by the patient to extent that it is possible for the patient with someone or something (such as a pulley) assisting him to complete the motion. (The patient has partial voluntary motion in the extremity.)

3. <u>Passive (R.O.M.)</u>: Motion is initiated and carried through by someone other than the patient or by the healthy part of the patient's body (e.g., a hemiplegic patient can use his unaffected arm to give passive R.O.M. to his affected arm). The patient usually has little or no voluntary motion of the affected extremity.

<u>Scoliosis</u>: See Chapter PHYSICAL DISABILITIES.

<u>Semi-Ambulatory</u>: The classification given to a patient who is able to be out of bed only a few hours a day. This classification is usually given to cardiac and tuberculosis patients who must gradually rebuild their strength but still need many hours of rest.

<u>Short-Term Patient</u>: A person who is ill or disabled for a brief period of time. In terms of the national averages for length of stay in hospitals, under eight days may be considered short-term. The extent of the illness and the length of treatment time required determine whether or not the patient is classified as short-term.

<u>Spasm</u>: An involuntary, sudden movement or convulsive muscular contraction.

<u>Spasticity</u>: Hypertension of muscles causing stiff and awkward movements; the result of upper motor neuron lesion (damage to the brain cell).

<u>Stroke</u>: See Chapter GERONTOLOGY.

<u>Superior</u>: Pertaining to the top of a body.

<u>Sympathetic Nervous System</u>: See Chapter GENERAL TERMINOLOGY.

<u>Symptomatic</u>: Due to organic causes.

<u>Therapeutic</u>: See Chapter GENERAL TERMINOLOGY.

<u>Therapeutics</u>: See Chapter GENERAL TERMINOLOGY.

<u>Thrombus</u>: A blood clot obstructing a blood vessel or a cavity of the heart.

<u>Traction</u>: Act of drawing or pulling tight.

<u>Trauma</u>: A wound or injury.

<u>Treatment</u>: See Chapter GENERAL TERMINOLOGY.

<u>Tremor</u>: A continuous quivering or shaking motion of part of the body.

Urinary Appliances:

1. Catheter: This is an artificial tube inserted into the bladder via the abdomen or through the urethra for the purposes of urine drainage when the nerves to this area are damaged. The tube is usually attached to a leg bag attached to the leg and the person can periodically empty this during the day. Because the tube is a foreign object, there is the possibility of infection which necessitates drinking plenty of fluids, thus diluting the urine and passing it before it has a chance to be infected.

2. Ileac Diversion: Often referred to as ileostomy. This is a surgical operation whereby a small part of the small intestine is cut out, attached to the ureters (the two tubes from the respective kidneys which drain urine into the bladder) and brought out the right side of the abdomen, thus forming a pouch and conduit for urine, bypassing the bladder. This operation is often done as a means against recurring bladder infections or as a preventive measure against them. The intestinal tract is normally filled with bacteria and therefore resistant to them. By using a piece of intestine as an artificial bladder, the chances for infection are reduced. A drainage appliance is attached over the stoma, usually glued to the skin. Some individuals may have to change this only once every two-three weeks; others may have trouble with it every couple of days. The bag is then cleaned, the skin cleaned and dried, and then the bag is reattached by glue and adhesive strips in most cases.

3. Colostomy: This is a similar operation, but this time the bowel is not removed, but rather taken directly to the surface and the feces empties into a similar type of bag.

4. Condoms: Some males will use just a simple condom attached over the penis and attached to a tube and drainage bag. There are a number of different types.

Ventrical: Pertaining to the undersurface of a body.

Vertigo: Sensation of dizziness; a whirling motion of oneself or of external objects. Can be caused by: cerebral anemia or congestion, gastric irritation, eyestrain, uterine disease, constipation, etc.

Weed System: See Chapter GENERAL TERMINOLOGY.

Wernicke's Syndrome: Resulting from Vitamin B deficiency in alcoholism; characterized by disturbed vision, memory loss, confusion, mind wandering, stupors, and sometimes coma.

Chapter IV

MENTAL RETARDATION

Ability Grouping: Subdivision on a group into smaller groups based on similar performances on tests, physical tasks, or other observable and measurable behavior; often used to better facilitate learning and cooperation.

Acrocephaly: A disorder characterized by anterior pointing of the head.

Adaptive Behavior: See Chapter GENERAL TERMINOLOGY.

Alexia: Generally indicates serious reading difficulty in which the individual is unable to read more than a few lines with understanding.

Anencephaly: Partial or complete absence of the cerebrum, cerebellum, and flat bones of the skull.

Anophthalmia: Congenital absence of one or both eyes.

Anoxia: Insufficient supply of oxygen content in the blood resulting in inadequate functioning of tissue, i.e., brain tissue.

Apert's Syndrome: A type of retardation characterized by vertical lengthening of the head, jutting jaw, bulging eyes, and webbed hands and feet.

Associative Learning: When one stimulus is experienced, a second tends to be recalled.

Autism: See Chapter PSYCHIATRIC DISABILITIES.

Baseline: The usual level of functioning on an individual prior to treatment.

Behavior Disorder: See Chapter GENERAL TERMINOLOGY.

Behavior Modification: See Chapter GENERAL TERMINOLOGY.

Behaviorism: See Chapter GENERAL TERMINOLOGY.

Brain Damaged: See Chapter GENERAL TERMINOLOGY.

Causes of Mental Retardation:

1. Infections--rubella and syphilis which are usually prenatal.

2. Intoxications--various drugs taken by the mother or maternal disorders which affect the unborn fetus, such as industrial chemicals or diabetes.

3. Trauma or physical injuries--prenatal hypoxia, mechanical injuries at birth, hemorrhaging, anemia, also postnatal shock, anemia and prolonged unconsciousness.

4. Metabolism or nutrition--lipid storage disorders, carbohydrate disorders, amino acid disorders, mineral disorders, endocrine disorders, etc.

5. Gross Brain Diseases--various heredogeneric disorders.

6. Chromosomal Disorders--Down's Syndrome.

7. Gestational Disorders--pre- and post-maturity.

8. Psychiatric Disorders--psychosis.

9. Environmental Differences--sensory deprivation.

Cerebral Palsy: See Chapter PHYSICAL DISABILITIES.

Cretinism: Congenital overactive thryoid with resultant mental retardation, delayed skeletal maturation, dry and cold extremities, and a large protruding tongue.

Cultural Deprivation: A condition in which there is insufficient appropriate stimulation in the total environment to allow for the teaching of skills needed to cope with the general environment.

DeLange's Syndrome: Severely retarded individuals of small stature, with bushy eyebrows, turned-up nose, wide upper lip, and skeletal abnormalities.

Dementia: An obsolete term referring to a general mental deterioration due to organic or emotional factors.

Dependent Mentally Retarded: A mentally retarded individual requiring continuing supervision or assistance in all of his daily functioning.

Developmental Disability: See Chapter GENERAL TERMINOLOGY.

Developmental Period: Before the age of 18; mental retardation originates during this period. I.Q. testing levels off after this age.

Domiciliary Care: The provision of living quarters and personal services and care for persons who need 24-hour supervision.

Down's Syndrome: Common form of mental retardation in which the individual has an extra chromosome; characterized by broad nose, slanting eyes, protruding large tongue, open mouth, square shaped ears, large muscles, broad, short skull, and often congenital heart disease. Also known as mongolism.

Dull Normal Intelligence: At or near the lower limits of average intellectual ability, i.e., between 85-90 I.Q.

Dyslexia: See Chapter GENERAL MEDICAL TERMINOLOGY.

Echolalia: The senseless, non-cognitive repetition of a word or sentence just spoken by another person.

Educable Mentally Retarded (EMR): Sometimes referred to as EMH (Educable mentally handicapped). Because of retarded intellectual development as determined by recognized standardized tests, are incapable of being educated profitably and efficiently through ordinary classroom instruction but whose intellectual ability would indicate a degree of scholastic attainment with benefit of special methods, materials, and facilities. I.Q. is 50-75 on standard tests. Sometimes known as "moron." Generally the EMR adult can function fairly independently in the community.

Elective Mutism: A refusal to speak independent of intellectual endowment occasionally found in retarded children.

Encephalitis: See Chapter GENERAL MEDICAL TERMINOLOGY.

Endogenous: Retarded due to genetic makeup.

Enrichment: A planned program with the intent to increase the rate of individual learning by provided additional experiences.

Epilepsy: See Chapter GENERAL MEDICAL TERMINOLOGY.

Exceptional Children: Those who deviate significantly from the average in physique, sensory acuity intelligence, social conformity, emotional development, or learning; sometimes used synonomously with mentally retarded.

Exogenous: Retarded due to brain damage, social deprivation, an other factors outside of genetic makeup.

Extended Care: Prolonged or continued supervision, care, custody, protection, etc. of an individual usually considered in contrast to active treatment.

Familial Mental Deficiency: Obsolete term for a type of retardation in which there appears to be a family history of borderline intelligence or mild retardation and poor accomplishments in society, academic retardation, poor work history, and often found with adverse postnatal environment, low birth weights, and premature deliveries.

Feebleminded: Obsolete term used to describe individuals of limited intelligence; generally associated with a mild degree of mental retardation.

Friedreich's Ataxia: A progressive disorder usually resulting in death by age 30; carried by recessive genes with manifestations of stumbling, ataxia, loss of position sense, etc.

Frolich's Syndrome: Obesity, understature, and deferred sexual development as a result of some pituitary dysfunction.

Grand Mal Epilepsy: Seizures characterized by generalized tonic and clonic movements of the extremities and resulting loss of consciousness.

Guardian: An individual (other than a guardian ad litem, q.v.) who has legal control and management of the person, or of the property or estate, or of both the person and the property, of a ward.

Guardian Al Litem: An individual appointed to represent a ward in a particular legal proceeding without control over either the ward's person or his estate.

Guardian of the Person: A guardian appointed to see that the ward has proper care and protective supervision in keeping with his needs.

Guardian of the Property: A guardian appointed to see that the financial affairs of the ward are handled in his best interests.

Habeas Corpus: A legal document that brings into court a person held in custody (e.g., in a mental hospital) to determine whether the custody is legal.

Halfway House: See Chapter GENERAL TERMINOLOGY.

High-risk Children: Those with apparent developmental lags, and those with early signs of sensorimotor or health problems or neuromuscular dyscoordination.

Hydrocephalis: Increased accumulation of fluid in the protective layers of the brain, causing an enlarged head, face disproportionately small, eyes hidden in sockets and turned upward. May result from developmental anomalies, infection, injury, or brain tumors often accompanied by retardation.

Hyperactive: Excessive, above the normal use of energy or power of the mind.

Hyperkinetic: See Chapter PSYCHIATRIC DISABILITIES.

Hypertrophy: See Chapter GENERAL MEDICAL TERMINOLOGY.

Hypoactive: Slow, sluggish movement; less than usual use of energy or normal power of the mind. Apparent in the mentally retarded, brain injured, and emotionally disturbed.

Idiocy: Complete congenital imbecility, resulting in severe, mental retardation; I.Q. scores below 25.

Idiot Savant: A person of low general intelligence with unusually high skill in some special tasks such as remembering dates, rote tasks, etc.

Illiteracy: Inability to read and/or write well enough for practical uses.

Imbecile: Obsolete term used to describe mental functioning of persons obtaining I.Q. scores ranging from 25-50; between moderate and severe levels of mental retardation.

Independent Living Skills: Skills related to independent social living; (e.g., handle money, count change, travel on public transportation).

Infantile Autism: See autism in Chapter PSYCHIATRIC DISABILITIES.

Inheritance Pattern:

1. Autosomal dominant inheritance--only a single dose of gene must be affected to result in clinical manifestations. The trait will be found in one parent of either sex and in half the sons and half the daughters of an affected individual.

2. Autosomal recessive inheritance--both genes must be abnormal to result in clinical manifestations. Parents are generally clinically normal, while theoretically one-fourth of the offspring inherit the abnormal genetic factor from each parent and are affected; one-half are carriers like the parents; and one-fourth are normal.

3. X-linked inheritance--traits determined by genes carried on the X chromosome may be either recessive or dominant in the female, but in the male who has only one X chromosome the trait will always be expressed.

Intelligence Quotient (I.Q.): A number used to express the relative level of a person's intelligence; standard scores compared with tested individual's chronological age peers.

Learning Disabled: Shows special learning disorder in one or more areas of performance or learning which dramatically inhibits the achievement of a competency level commensurate with the level predicted by intelligence test data.

Legal Guardian: A guardian appointed by a court.

Life Support Care: Care necessary for some profoundly retarded individuals with major biomedical problems, i.e., requiring oxygen.

Mainstreaming: The concept of integrating various special needs children (physically handicapped, learning disabled, etc.) with normal children, to reinforce positive role identification.

Maternal Deprivation: A condition in which the infant receives insufficient, inconsistent, and/or inappropriate stimulation or care.

Measured Intelligence: Capacity to perceive and understand relationships as measured by a standardized general intelligence test such as the following:

1. Stanford-Binet Intelligence Scale

2. Wechsler Intelligence Scale for Children (WISC)

3. Wechsler Adult Intelligence Scale (WAIS)

4. Wechsler Preschool and Primary Scale of Intelligence (WPPSI)

5. Kuhlmann-Binet: An intelligence test which extends down to the four-month level.

Mental Age: Measured mental ability usually as determined by an intelligence test and as distinguished from the chronological age of the individual.

Mental Retardation: Significantly subaverage general intellectual functioning, which may be evident at birth or develop during childhood. Learning, adaptive behavior, social adjustment, and maturation are impaired. The degree of retardation is commonly measured in terms of I.Q.: borderline (83-68), mild (67-52), moderate (51-36), severe (35-20), and profound (under 20).

Microcephalic: Having an abnormally small head. Common in profound retardation.

Mild Mental Retardation: See "mental retardation."

Moderate Mental Retardation: See "mental retardation."

Mongolism: See "Down's Syndrome."

Moron: Obsolete term describing a person with mild mental retardation characterized by an I.Q. of 50-75. The preferred term is educable mentally retarded.

Multiply Handicapped: Refers to a person who has more than one handicap, the combination of which makes it difficult for him to benefit from a normal education program.

Multisensory Learning: A technique used to facilitate learning that employs a combination of sense modalities at the same time, i.e., sight, tactile, taste, audition.

Natural Guardian: A parent lawfully in control of the person of his minor child; natural guardianship terminates when the child reaches legal adulthood.

Need Achievement: A concept measuring motivation for success in specific areas, based on the individual's fantasy when presented certain pictures.

Nongraded Class: A small school class providing special education opportunities for handicapped persons needing individualized learning programs and group activities; grouped according to chronological age and ability or by disability (physically disabled, learning disabled).

Normalization Principle: The principle of helping the developmentally disabled to obtain a nearly normal existence, making available to them conditions of everyday life that are as close as possible to the norms and patterns of the mainstream of society.

Perceptual Disorder: A cerebral impairment of the awareness of visual, auditory, or haptic stimuli.

Performance Test: Generally a non-verbal standardized test of intelligence and/or physical ability which generally requires the use and manipulation of physical objects and the application of physical and manual skills.

Personal Adjustment Training: Adjustment to work rather than a specific skill through exposure to a real work situation; stresses personal and social skills needed to get along, work tolerance, appropriate work habits, and emotional stability in responding to work pressures.

Play Therapy: See Chapter GENERAL TERMINOLOGY.

Profound Mental Retardation: See "mental retardation."

Proprioception: See Chapter GENERAL MEDICAL TERMINOLOGY.

Psychogenic Mental Retardation: Subaverage mental functioning and deficits in adaptive behavior with no known pathological origins.

Psychomotor Seizures: Seizures with semipurposeful movements occurring during a period of altered consciousness; includes grasping movements of the hand, smacking of the lips, irrelevant speech, and inappropriate behavior.

Psychopharmacology: See Chapter PSYCHIATRIC DISABILITIES.

Residential Facility: See Chapter GERONTOLOGY.

Respite Care: Services provided for the care of an individual through temporary separation from his family for short periods of time on a regular or intermittent basis for the purpose of relieving the family of his care; serves to (1) meet planned or emergency needs; (2) restore physical or mental well-being; and (3) initiate training procedures in or out of the home.

Rh Incompatibility: The mother has Rh negative blood and the fetus has Rh positive blood causing antibody formation in the mother, which affects the fetus. This may cause the destruction of Rh positive red blood cells resulting in abortions, stillbirths, or possible mental retardation.

Rubella: Called German measles; when occurring in the pregnant mother, the infection may affect the fetus causing deafness, cataracts, cardiamalformations, and/or mental retardation.

Self-help Skills: Skills such as toileting, grooming, dressing, feeding, etc.

Sensory Deprivation: One or more of the major senses (e.g., vision, hearing) are so impaired as to restrict the use of the sense; intellectual retardation will occur if compensations are not made for the reduced sensory input.

Shaping: Development of new behaviors through systematic plans of reinforcement for successive approximations of the specific behavioral goal.

Slow Learner: A child with social and academic behavior less than usual age level standards.

Social Inadequacy: The inability of the retarded person to function effectively in a social setting.

Special Class: A group of children assigned to a particular class on the basis of some disability (e.g., educable mental retardation, emotional disturbance) and given instruction by teachers with specific training.

Special Olympics: See Chapter GENERAL TERMINOLOGY.

Stereotyped Behaviors: Complex, repetitive movements which appear to have no function (e.g., repetitive hand movements, rocking, object twirling, or head banging) common with severely retarded individuals and congenitally blind persons.

Trainable Mentally Retarded (TMR): Those individuals below the age of 21 who, because of retarded intellectual development are incapable of being educated properly and efficiently through ordinary classroom instruction or special education facilities for the educable mentally retarded children, but who may be expected to benefit from training in a setting designed to further their social adjustment and economic usefulness in their homes or in a sheltered environment. These children would obtain I.Q. scores between 35 and 50 on recognized standardized individual tests of intelligence. Sometimes known as trainable mentally handicapped (TMH) and/or "imbecile."

Training: Services with an emphasis on learning those skills universally needed to function at a minimum level as part of society.

Transfer of Training: The effect of learning one thing upon the learning of another; a task thought to be more difficult for the mentally retarded child.

1. Positive transfer—learning one skill helps in learning the second skill.

2. Negative transfer—learning one skill interferes with learning another skill.

Underachiever: A person who does not perform in specified ways as well as expected from previous known records; a person who doesn't accomplish as much as expected from his measured intelligence.

Chapter V

GERONTOLOGY

Amnesia: See Chapter GENERAL MEDICAL TERMINOLOGY.

Angina Pectoris: Severe pain in the region of the heart, radiating to the left shoulder, and sometimes down the left arm. The face is either pale, ashen (gray), or livid (red), the brow is bathed in sweat. Dyspnea (difficult breathing) is often noted; the pulse is variable, usually tense and quick. Blood pressure is raised during an attack. Attacks will last from a few seconds to several minutes. Common in the elderly.

Aphasia: The inability to express oneself properly through speech. The main types of aphasia are:

1. Expressive: the inability to express onself by talking or writing; also known as motor aphasia.

2. Receptive: the inability to understand either spoken or written word.

3. Mixed: a combination of expressive and receptive aphasia (global).

4. Nominal Aphasia: like a memory defect in that the person understands what is said to him, can read and can talk, but is unable to remember the names of various objects.

Arthritis: See Chapter GENERAL MEDICAL TERMINOLOGY.

A.S.H.D.: Arteriosclerotic Heart Disease: Hardening of the vessels of the heart.

Brain Damaged: See Chapter GENERAL MEDICAL TERMINOLOGY.

C.V.A.: See Chapter GENERAL MEDICAL TERMINOLOGY.

Disoriented: Confused as to time and place; sometimes name.

Extended Care Facility: A facility in which prolonged or continued supervision, care, custody, protection of the individual are provided.

Geriatrics: Branch of medicine dealing with the medical problems of the aging.

Gerontology: The study of the aging process and of aging persons in society. The types of aging are:

1. The mature type includes individuals who accept the facts of aging, adjust well to losses, are realistic about their past and present lives, and face death with relative equanimity.

2. The armored type includes persons who cling to middle-class behavior patterns, deny aging, keep as busy as ever, and manage to get along very well.

3. The "rocking chair" type, which is growing as society becomes more leisure-oriented, includes persons who accept passivity, sit and rock without feeling guilty about it.

Golden Age Clubs: Social or recreation clubs for older persons, operating under volunteer or non-professional leadership, and meeting not more than a few times a week.

Hemiplegia: Complete or partial paralysis of one side of the body.

Hypertension: High blood pressure.

Incontinence: See Chapter GENERAL MEDICAL TERMINOLOGY.

Intermediate Care Facility: A long-term health care facility providing basic care to residents needing moderate and periodic medical support and rehabilitation measures. They are not in need of 24-hour supervision and care.

Leisure Village: Special resident homes or garden apartments for the aging who can live independently; generally characterized by active recreation programs. They are usually expensive and therefore appeal to those who are financially independent.

Long-term Health Care Facility: Residential home for aging and disabled who have suffered fairly serious mental or physical impairment and who are not able to live independently in the community. Some degree of custodial care is usually necessary; sometimes called "nursing homes" or "convalescent homes."

"Meal on Wheels" Program: An effort on the part of local senior citizens groups (e.g., Council on Aging) to provide one hot meal a day to homebound senior citizens.

Organic Brain Syndrome (OBS): A disorder caused by or associated with impairment of brain tissue function. It may be manifested by disorientation, loss of memory, and impairment of the ability to learn, comprehend, calculate, and exercise judgment. May be psychotic or non-psychotic, mild, moderate, or severe. Simple drunkenness is an example of non-psychotic OBS, and senile dementia of the psychotic type.

Reality Orientation: A technique developed by Dr. Folsom to reorient confused individuals; a constant awareness of present reality, i.e., time, day, place, name, etc.

Residential Facility: A facility that provides twenty-four hour programming services, including residential or domiciliary services, directed to enhancing the health, welfare, and development of persons that are aging, mentally retarded, or possessing other developmental disabilities. While the facility must provide twenty-four hour programming for residents, in accordance with their needs, it need not itself operate any programs or services other than residential or domiciliary care.

Senile: Pertaining to growing old or to be aged; associated with memory loss.

Senility: Physical and mental infirmity of old age. Often misused and overused.

✓ Senior Citizen Centers: Diversified programs of activity for the aging, conducted by professional staff members from various types of municipal agencies (e.g., municipal recreation), and meeting for a substantial number of hours per week.

✓ Sheltered Care Facility: Provision of personal care and assistance, supervision, and a suitable activities program. Provisions are made for medical care as necessary. Such facilities are for individuals who do not need nursing care, but do need personal care, assistance, supervision, in meeting their daily personal needs.

Sheltered Workshop: See Chapter GENERAL MEDICAL TERMINOLOGY.

✓ Skilled Care Facility: A long-term health care facility that provides skilled nursing care, continuous skilled nursing observations, restorative nursing, and other services under professional direction with frequent medical supervision. Such facilities are provided for patients who need the type of care and treatment required during the post acute phase of illness or during recurrences of sym toms in long-term illness.

✓ Stroke: CVA - Cerebral Vascular Accident; this refers to stoppage of circulation to part of the brain either by the blood vessel bursting or being narrowed enough to deprive the area of blood. This generally partially paralyzes one side of the body and also may affect speech, judgment, memory, etc. The majority of strokes occur in older people, but no age group is exempt.

✓ Telecare Program: A volunteer program to provide daily contact to shut-in or home-bound senior citizens via the telephone.

Well-being Clinic: A clinic for retirement and pre-retirement age individuals where they can receive medical and psychiatric checkups and treatment, counseling, and activity therapies.

Chapter VI

PHYSICAL DISABILITIES

Adventitious Disabilities: Physically disabling conditions that are acquired after birth by traumatic or chronic events.

Apparatus: Wheelchairs, braces, crutches, adaptive devices, etc.

Architectural Barrier: Physical barriers which make it difficult or impossible for the physically disabled to move about freely with other people, such as: stairs, narrow doorways, soft pathways, high drinking fountains, and sinks, etc.

Ataxia: See Chapter GENERAL MEDICAL TERMINOLOGY.

Auditory Disorder: Impaired reception and interpretation of sound.

Amputees: Loss of limb, either congenitally or due to an accident. Many of these individuals use artificial limbs (prosthetics).

BEH: Bureau of Education for the Handicapped; a section of the Department of Health, Education, and Welfare (HEW); advocates the training of professionals to deal with the special needs of handicapped children.

Cerebral Palsy (C.P.): A disability due to damage of centers of the brain before or during birth resulting in imperfect control of the muscles and marked especially by muscular incoordination, spastic paralysis, and speech disturbances. It is estimated that more than half of the cerebral palsied are mentally retarded. The types of C.P. include:

1. Spastic: characterized by jerky and uncertain movements and tightly contracting muscles.

2. Athetoid: typically showing uncontrolled, sprawling, muscular functioning.

3. Rigid: extremely tight muscles and limited, resistive movement.

4. Tremor: uncontrollably shaking limbs.

Chronic Disabilities: Usually refers to those resulting from diseases or conditions that may be slow-moving and progressive or in an arrested state, i.e., where the progression or worsening has temporarily or permanently ceased.

COHI-MH: See Chapter GENERAL MEDICAL TERMINOLOGY.

Congenital Deafness: Individual is born deaf due to prenatal or natal nerve destruction or injury, illness of the mother during pregnancy, incompatible Rh factors, or prolonged labor.

Cystic Fibrosis: A disease of the very young involving the endocrine glands, resulting in pancreatic insufficiency, chronic pulmonary disease, abnormally high sweat electrolyte levels, and sometimes cirrhosis of the liver; a fatal disease.

Decubitus Ulcer: See Chapter GENERAL MEDICAL TERMINOLOGY.

Diabetes Mellitus: Disease in which the body is unable to ingest starches and sugars due to an inadequate supply of naturally produced insulin.

Diplegia: Paralysis affecting the same parts on both sides of the body; a bilateral paralysis.

Dystonis Musculorum Deformans: A slightly progressive disease affecting part of the brain which mediates and controls movement. Because of this, the person will move with slow, difficult movements and may be prone to a flexed, bent-over posture.

Friederich's Ataxia: See Chapter GENERAL MEDICAL TERMINOLOGY.

Functionally Blind: The individual cannot read printed materials or distinguish figures on television.

Glaucoma: Hardening of the eyeball and blindness resulting from abnormal pressure within the eyeball due to poor circulation of fluid.

Handicapped Child: One who cannot play, learn, work, or do the things other children his age can do or is hindered in achieving his full physical, mental, and social potentialities, whether by a disability which is initially small but potentially handicappling, or by a serious impairment involving several areas of function with the probability of life-long impairment.

Hearing Impaired: Deaf and hard of hearing--deaf individuals are those whose hearing loss is so severe that they are unable to hear speech unless it is amplified. These children generally have a loss of 71 decibels or more in both ears. Hard of hearing individuals are those who are able to understand and learn speech and language with adaptations but whose hearing may not be sufficient to enable them to learn adequately in the regular school class, even with the assistance of a special teacher. These individuals generally have a hearing loss from 40-71 decibels in the better ear.

Hemicorporectomy: Amputation of the lower half of the body, due to disease or injury, e.g., cancer or injury.

Hemiplegia: See Chapter GERONTOLOGY.

Hyperopia: Farsightedness; poor vision up close.

Legally Blind: A visual acuity of 20/200 or less or a visual field of 20%; the individual cannot see as well at 20 feet what the normal individual can see at 200 feet.

Legg-Perthes Disease: A diminished blood supply to the hip causing the bone to become shorter and the head of the thigh bone to become flat. Given time to heal by keeping weight off the hip usually corrects the problem, but this can take from 12-36 months.

Leukemia: A fatal disease characterized by increased white blood cells in the blood stream.

Loss of Muscle Movement:

    1. Monoplegia: total or partial paralysis of one extremity.

2. <u>Hemiplegia</u>: total or partial paralysis of one side of the body.

3. <u>Paraplegia</u>: total or partial paralysis of the lower extremities and/or paralysis of parts or part of the trunk. This means the person will have full function of their arms, neck, shoulders, and hands.

4. <u>Quadriplegia</u>: refers to paralysis in all four extremities and the trunk. However, the upper extremities and neck are never totally paralyzed. The spinal column has nerves existing from it innervating the muscles. In general, the lower the injury to the spinal cord, the more function is left. A person injured in the neck may be only able to bend his neck, shrug his shoulders, raise his arm, and bend his elbow, whereas a person injured in the low back may only suffer paralysis in the lower parts of his legs. The nerves to the bowel and bladder, unfortunately, exit very low, and almost always these are affected.

    The persons with high involvement may have respiratory problems and the degree of help they will need will vary. Persons who have full use of their upper extremities can do most everything themselves. There is a loss of sensation at the level of injury also, so pressure sores are a potential problem. A regular diet and plenty of fluids are very important to these people.

<u>Mapping</u>: One's ability to chart a course enabling him to move safely, effectively, and comfortably from one place to another within his immediate environment by using cuse such as size, shape, odor, and landmarks.

<u>Medically Approved Recreation</u>: The broad approval of recreation activities by a physician.

<u>Medical Clearance</u>: The approval from a doctor from an individal or group to partake in some recreation activity. This procedure is used to obtain premission for patients to go to some event or partake in activities.

<u>Medical Limitations</u>: The restrictions imposed upon a patient by medical authorities. These restrictions are based on the extent of the illness and/or treatment plan.

<u>Meningitis</u>: Inflammation of the membranes surrounding the brain and spinal cord. Can result in various types of brain damage.

<u>Microcephalus</u>: Having a small head.

<u>Mobile Nonabmulatory</u>: Unable to walk without assistance, but able to move from place to place with the use of devices such as walkers, crutches, wheelchairs, wheeled platforms, etc.

<u>Multiple Sclerosis</u>: There is an insulating layer of fatty substance over the brain and spinal cord, serving much like insulation over an electric wire and insuring free passage of impulses; in the human, transmission of nervous impulses to the muscles. In Multiple Sclerosis (M.S.), this insulating layer for some reason breaks down, sclerotic patches occur in the brain and spinal cord and this interferes with the proper transmission of nervous impulses. The resultant course of this disease is one of "ups" and "downs", but usually progressing slowly downhill. Because of the damage to the nervous system, coordination, strength, speech, eyesight--one or all may be compromised. This is a rather

bizarre disease, occurring much more in the northern area of the United States, Canada, and the Scandinavian countries. It is the crippler of young adults, usually striking the ages of 20-40.

Multiphy Handicapped: Refers to an individual who has more than one handicap, the combination of which makes him unable to benefit from a normal education program.

Muscular Dystrophy (M.D.): There are several different types of muscular dystrophy, which is a genetic hereditary disease which results in a progressive wasting away of muscle.

1. Pseudohypertrophic: The wasted away muscle is replaced by fibrous tissue and fat. This type is transmitted from mother to son. The person may appear to have big muscular calves, buttocks, and shoulders. This disease affects primarily the trunk, shoulders, hips, calves, neck and face muscles. Many die before they are 20 years old, not directly from M.D. but due to the lessening of respiratory functioning. The muscles controlling coughing are affected and thus mucous secretions stay in the lungs where it is warm and moist, creating a condition very conducive to infection and pneumonia. It is most important to guard against colds.

2. Amytonia Congenita (Oppenheim's Disease): This is a non-progressive disorder in which there is a deficiency of the motor cells in the spinacl cord which sends the message to the muscles. Because of this deficiency, the muscles are not fully innervated with the resultant weakness and lack of muscle tone. Because the person becomes older and bigger, he or she becomes even weaker, but the basic deficit does not get worse, however, it may appear to, due to body growth. As the person reaches full growth, the condition tends to stabilize. The same respiratory precautions as in M.D. should be followed in caring for these people.

3. Progressive Spinal Muscular Atrophy (Werdnig-Hoffman's Disease): The basic cause here is the same as in Amytonia Congenita, but here the nerve cells deteriorate and the disease is progressive, much like M.D. This is also hereditary and begins during early childhood. It first affects the hips and thighs and later spreads to the extremities.

4. Perineal Muscular Atrophy (Charcot-Marie Tooth Disease): This is a form of the above; also with hereditary tendencies and usually occurring in children. It involves progressive weakness of the distal muscles of the arms and feet--near the ankles and hands.

5. Myotonia Congenita (Thompson's Disease): This is a rare inherited disease characterized by an excess of muscle tone, whereby the muscles are very rigid and unyielding with attacks of muscle spasm occurring.

6. Limb-girdle M.D.: This involves progressive weakness and wasting of mainly the lower limbs, and usually begins after the age of 10.

7. Facial-Scapular-Humeral Dystrophy: This type of dystrophy usually affects adults and involves the muscles of the face, shoulder blades, arms and shoulders.

Myelitis: Inflammation of the spinal cord.

Myopia: Nearsightedness; inability to focus distant objects.

Neurological Disorders: Disease or injury to the nervous system.

Nephritis: Inflammation of the kidney.

Neuritis: Inflammation of a nerve.

Non-ambulatory: See Chapter GENERAL MEDICAL TERMINOLOGY.

NRA: National Rehabilitation Association.

NWAA: National Wheelchair Athletic Association; originated by Ben Lipton in 1956.

NWBA: National Wheelchair Basketball Association; originated by Tim Nugent in 1949.

Orthopedics: Branch of medicine that deals with treatment of disorders involving locomotor structures of the body, especially the skeleton, joints, muscles and fascia.

Osteomyelitis: Bone infection.

Paralympics: Olympic games held often in conjunction with the International Olympics for handicapped athletes.

Paraplegic: A person with paralysis of lower portion of the body and both legs.

Parkinson's Disease: A chronic nervous disease characterized by a fine, slowly spreading tremor, muscular weakness and rigidity.

Partially Blind: A visual acuity of 20/70 to 20/200. The individual has difficulty seeing at 20 feet what the normally sighted individual can see at 70 to 200 feet.

Physical Disability: Relates to the physical degeneration or loss to an individual that may have been caused by congenital or adventitious factors. Often used concomitantly with "physical handicap "

Physically Handicapped: Same as physically disabled.

Physical Therapy: See Chapter GENERAL TERMINOLOGY.

Poliomyelitis (Polio): Caused by a virus that affects the part of the spinal cord that sends out the motor message to the muscle. It does not affect the sensory part. The amount and degree of damage depends upon which parts of the spinal cord were affected, ranging from involvement of one leg to involvement of all extremities and the trunk. The muscles are thus deprived of their nerve output and waste away. Once the damage has occurred, it is non-reversible and yet non-progressive.

Prosthesis: Replacement of a missing part by an artificial substitute; an artificial organ or part.

Quadriplegic: A person with paralysis affecting the body from the neck down.

Rheumatic Heart Disease: Permanent damage to the heart valves as a result of rheumatic fever.

Rickets: Bent, distorted, and enlarged bones due to a lack of vitamin D in childhood.

Rubella: See Chapter MENTAL RETARDATION.

Rigid: Constant resistance to movement. The spastic muscle will "give" and relax when it is moved to some degree, but rigidity means the muscles are generally very tight and stiff.

Scoliosis: A condition in which the spinal column is curved toward one side instead of normally straight. Severe cases can affect respiratory mechanism. Sometimes occurs in people with muscular dystrophy, or polio due to muscular imbalance in the back.

Semi-ambulatory: See Chapter GENERAL MEDICAL TERMINOLOGY.

Severe Handicap: See Chapter GENERAL TERMINOLOGY.

Spastic: Indicates there is an abnormal resistance to movement-tight muscles. This person will have a tendency to develop muscular contractures because of the brain lesion which interferes with free movement.

Speech Handicapped: Speech which has been diagnosed by a speech therapist as deviating or differing from average or normal speech to the extent that it hinders adequate communication and requires specialized instruction for improvement or correction of the handicaps.

Spina Bifida: "Bifid" means short, thus a "short spine." This is a congenital malformation of the spinal cord and the supporting vertebral column causing the spinal cord to herniate through causing paralysis below this point. Most of the time this occurs in the low back and the person will have a surgical scar and/or remnants of the "bif." Most people usually have some use of their upper legs and are able to walk with crutches and/or braces. The nerves to the bowel and bladder are always impaired and the person may have a type of urinary receptacle, use suppositories or be on a regular time schedule for bowel movements. Many have slightly enlarged heads due to the trauma to the spinal cord, upsetting the balance of spinal fluid and causing an increase of pressure in the head. This is known as HYDROCEPHALUS and also occurs apart from Spina Bifida. The spinal cord and brain are bathed in spinal fluid which is produced and reabsorbed into the bloodstream in the brain. This fluid circulates up and down bathing the brain and the spinal cord. Due to congenital or developmental defects in this system, blockage of channels, etc., an increase of pressure and a resultant increase in skull size occurs. This can cause neurological and mental damage and the degree of damage will again vary a great deal.

Traumatic Disabilities: Caused by a fast-moving or critical incident such as accident, assault, war, or other similar episodes.

Urinary Appliances: See Chapter GENERAL MEDICAL TERMINOLOGY.

V.A. Hospitals: Veterans Administration Hospitals; utilized for the treatment of war veterans. In 1945 the V.A. hospitals organized Recreation Services for their hospitalized veterans.

Visionally Impaired (Blind/partially sighted): A person with a visual handicap who will be unable to use print as his reading medium is considered to be functionally blind. Special aids will be essential to education. Visual acuity is 20/200 or less in the better eye with the best possible correction or a restriction in the field of vision to an angle subtending an arc of 20 degrees or less. He falls within the definition of blindness, although he may have some useful vision.

Wheelchair Sports: Organized athletics for disabled athletes. The rules are slightly modified to enable handicapped individuals to participate in most sports events.

Chapter VII

PSYCHIATRIC DISABILITIES

<u>Acting Out</u>: Expression of unconscious emotional conflicts or feelings of hostility or love in actions that the individual does not consciously know are related to such conflicts or feelings. May be harmful or, in controlled situations, therapeutic (e.g., in children's play therapy, adult gestalt therapy, psychodrama, etc.).

<u>Adaptive Behavior</u>: See Chapter GENERAL TERMINOLOGY.

<u>Affective Disorder</u>: Any mental disorder in which a disturbance of feeling or emotion is predominant. This is a broad concept that includes depressive neurosis (see under neurosis), the major affective disorders, and psychotic depressive reaction.

<u>Aggressive Behavior</u>: Hostile behavior used to express strong feelings about certain situations. Aggressive behavior may in some cases be an attention-getting device. In other cases it may be a reaction to a hostile environment in which one is expected to perform beyond his capabilities.

<u>Alcoholic Paranoia</u>: See Chapter GENERAL MEDICAL TERMINOLOGY.

<u>Ambivalence</u>: The coexistence of two opposing drives, desires, feelings or emotions toward the same person, object or goal. These may be conscious or partly conscious; or one side of the feelings may be unconscious (e.g., love and hate toward the same person).

<u>Ambulatory Schizophrenia</u>: An unofficial term for a person with schizophrenia who functions sufficiently well that he generally does not require hospitalization. If in a hospital, he is kept on open wards or allowed the complete freedom of the community.

<u>Amenorrhoa</u>: A feeling of impotence.

<u>Anorexia Nervosa</u>: A syndrome marked by severe and prolonged inability to eat, with marked weight loss, amenorrhea (impotence), and other symptoms resulting from emotional conflict. Most frequently encountered in young females.

<u>Antabuse</u>: Disulfiram, a drug used in aversive treatment of alcoholism. It blocks the normal metabolism of alcohol and produces increased blood concentrations of acetaldehydes, which cause very unpleasant reactions, including pounding of the heart, shortness of breath, nausea, and vomiting.

<u>Anxiety</u>: Apprehension, tension, or uneasiness that stems from the anticipation of danger danger, the source of which is largely unknown or unrecognized. Primarily of intrapsychic origin, in distinction to fear, which is the emotional response to a consciously recognized and usually edternal threat or danger. Anxiety and fear are accompanied by similar physiologic changes. May be regarded as pathologic when present to such extent as to interfere with effectiveness in living, achievement of desired goals or satisfactions, or reasonable emotional comfort.

Autism: Absorption in fantasy to the exclusion of interest in reality. Mental introversion in which the attention or interest is fastened within one's ego; a self-centered mental state from which reality tends to be excluded.

Autistic Child: In child psychiatry, a child who responds chiefly to inner thoughts, who does not relate to his environment, his overall functioning is immature and he often appears retarded.

Behavior Disorder: See Chapter GENERAL TERMINOLOGY.

Behaviorism: See Chapter GENERAL TERMINOLOGY.

Behavioral Psychology: A belief that all human behavior is the result of learned associations of stimulus and response that the individual has been conditioned to adopt. Behavior is seen as a response to external pressures, and therefore adaptive.

Behavior Therapy: See Chapter GENERAL TERMINOLOGY.

Catalepsy: A generalized condition of diminished responsiveness usually characterized by trance-like states. May occur in organic or psychological disorders, or under hypnosis.

Catatonic State (catatonia): A state characterized by immobility with muscular rigidity or inflexibility and at times by excitability. Often a symptom of schizophrenia.

Catharsis: (1) The healthful (therapeutic) release of ideas through a "talking out" or acting out of conscious material accompanied by the appropriate emotional reaction. (2) The release into awareness of repressed (i.e., "forgotten") material from the unconscious.

Character Disorder: A personality disorder manifested by a chronic and habitual pattern of reaction that is maladaptive in that it is relatively inflexible, limits the optimal use of potentialities, and often provokes the very counter reactions from the environment that the subject seeks to avoid. In contrast to symptoms of neurosis, character traits are typically egosyntonic (not harmonious in interpersonal relationships).

Chemotherapy: Treatment of mental, physical, and social malfunctioning by means of drugs.

Closed Ward: A section of the hospital for very disturbed psychiatric or senile patients. This section is usually locked and is often referred to as a locked ward.

Closed Ward Patient: A patient in a section of the hospital for very disturbed mental or senile patients. The patients are usually on closed wards because they require custodial care as well as treatment.

Community Psychiatry: Recent movement to provide for psychiatric care in the community, thereby helping the patient to move toward adjustment and constructive living in their immediate environment. Emphasis is placed on treatment in the community, the utilization of clinic resources, day and night hospital units, crisis-oriented therapy, rehabilitation and aftercare, hospitalization in psychiatric units in general hospitals, earlier discharge, use of halfway houses, and the establishment of special programs for the mentally retarded, aged, alcoholics, and addicts. The education of the public becomes paramount in helping change community attitudes toward the mentally ill.

<u>Compensation</u>: Covering up weakness by emphasizing desirable traits or making up for frustration in one area by over-gratification in another.

<u>Conversion Reaction</u>: A defense mechanism, operating unconsciously, by which intrapsychic conflicts that would otherwise give rise to anxiety are, instead, given symbolic external expression. The repressed ideas or impulses, plus the psychologic defenses against them, are converted into a variety of somatic symptoms--(e.g., psychogenic paralysis of a limb that prevents its use for aggressive purposes).

<u>Crisis Intervention</u>: Treatment provided at the turning point of mental illness; at the most critical moment in the individual's illness appropriate treatment is provided to prevent the patient from harming himself or others. Treatment can be in the form of counseling, chemotherapy, hospitalization, etc.

<u>Defense Mechanism</u>: Unconscious intrapsychic processes that are employed to seek relief from emotional conflict and freedom from anxiety. Conscious efforts are frequently made for the same reasons, but true defense mechanisms are unconscious. Some of the common defense mechanisms are: compensation, conversion, denial, displacement, dissociation, idealization, identification, incorporation, introjection, projection, rationalization, reaction formation, regression, repression, sublimation, substitution, symbolization, and undoing.

<u>Deja Vu</u>: The sensation that what one is seeing has been seen before.

<u>Delirium</u>: A mental state characterized by confusion and altered, possibly fluctuating, consciousness. Delusions, illusions, hallucinations, and lability of emotions, particularly anxiety and fear, are often present.

<u>Delirium Tremens</u>: An acute and sometimes fatal disorder involving impairment of brain tissue; usually caused by withdrawal from excessive and unusually prolonged alcohol intake and manifested by tremors, frightening illusions, hallucinations, and sometimes convulsions.

<u>Delusion</u>: A false belief out of keeping with the individual's level of knowledge and his cultural group. The belief results from unconscious needs and is maintained against logical argument and despite objective contradictory evidence. Common delusions include:

1. <u>Delusions of grandeur</u>: Exaggerated ideas of one's importance or identity.

2. <u>Delusions of persecution</u>: Ideas that one has been singled out for persecution.

3. <u>Delusions of reference</u>: Incorrect assumption that certain casual or unrelated events or the behavior of others may apply to oneself.

<u>Denial</u>: A defense mechanism, operating unconsciously, used to resolve emotional conflict and allay anxiety by disavowing thoughts, feelings, wishes, needs, or external reality factors that are consciously intolerable.

Depression: A morbid sadness, dejection, or melancholy. To be differentiated from grief, which is realistic and proportionate to what has been lost. A depression may be a symptom of any psychiatric disorder or may constitute its principal manifestation. Neurotic depressions are differentiated from psychotic depressions in that they do not involve loss of capacity for reality testing. The major psychotic depressions include psychotic, depressive reaction and the variour major affective disorders.

Disease Model: Concept of mental illness that suggests that psychotic behavior unfolds inevitably from a defective psychological or neurological system that is contained in the person. Belief that mental illness is caused in much the same manner as a virus.

Displacement: Discharging pent-up feelings, usually of hostility, on objects less dangerous than those which initially surround the emotions.

Dissociation: A defense mechanism, operating unconsciously, through which emotional significance and affect are separated and detached from an idea, situation, or object. Dissociation may defer or postpone experiencing some emotional impact as, for example, in selective amnesia.

Dominance: (1) In psychiatry, an individual's disposition to play a prominent or controlling role in his interaction with others. (2) In neurology, the (normal) tendency of one half of the brain to be more important than the other in controlling behavior (cerebral dominance). (3) In genetics, the ability of one gene (dominant gene) to express itself in the phenotype of an individual, even though that gene is paired with another (recessive gene) that would have expressed itself in a different way.

Double Bind: A type of interaction, noted frequently in families with schizophrenic members, in which one person (often the mother) demands a response to a message containing mutually contradictory signals while the other (the schizophrenic son, for example) is unable either to comment on the incongruity or to escape from the situation (e.g., a mother tells her son to act like a man and express his opinion and when he does, she berates him as unloving and disloyal).

Drive: Basic urge, instinct, motivation; in psychiatry, a term currently preferred to avoid confusion with the more purely biological concept of instinct.

Dyssocial Behavior: In psychiatry, a diagnostic term for individuals who are not classifiable as anti-social personalities, but who are predatory and follow more or less criminal pursuits such as racketeers, dishonest gamblers, prostitutes, and dope peddlers. Sometimes called "sociopathic personalities."

Echolalia: The pathologic repetition by imitation of the speech of another. Sometimes seen in schizophrenia, catatonic type.

Ego: In psychoanalytic theory, one of the three major divisions in the model of the psychic apparatus, the others being the id and superego. The ego represents the sum of certain mental mechanisms, such as perception and memory, and specific defense mechanisms. The ego serves to mediate between the demands of primitive instinctual drives (the id), of internalized parental and social prohibitions (the superego), and of reality. The compromises between these forces achieved by the ego tend to resolve intrapsychic conflict and serve an adaptive and executive function. Psychiatric usage of the term should not be confused with common usage, which connotes "self-love" or "selfishness."

Ego Ideal: That part of the personality that comprises the aims and goals of the self; usually refers to the conscious or unconscious emulation of significant figures with whom the person has identified. The ego ideal emphasizes what one should be or do in contrast to what one should not be or do.

Existential Psychiatry (existentialism): A school of psychiatry that has evolved out of orthodox psychoanalytic thought and incorporates the ideas of such existentialists as Kierkegaard, Heidegger, Sartre, and others. It focues on the individual's subjective awareness of his style of existence, his intimate interactions with himself, his values, and his environment. Stress is placed on the way in which man experiences the phenomenological world about him and takes responsibility for his existence. Philosophically, the point of view is holistic and self-deterministic in contrast to biologically or culturally deterministic points of view.

Fantasy: An imagined sequence of events or mental images, (e.g., day dreams). Serves to express unconscious conflicts, to gratify unconscious wishes, or to prepare for anticipated future events.

Free Association: The psychoanalytic procedure which requires the patient to speak aloud his thought flow, word for word, without censorship, in an effort to understand repressed sources of anxiety.

Fugue: A major state of personality dissociation characterized by amnesia; may involve actual physical flight from the customary environment.

Galvanic Skin Response (GSR): The resistance of the skin to the passage of a weak electric current: an easily measured variable widely used in experimental studies as a measure of an individual's response to emotion-arousing stimuli.

Gestalt Therapy: See Chapter GENERAL TERMINOLOGY.

Grandiose: In psychiatry, exaggerated belief or claims of one's importance or identity; often manifested by delusions of great wealth, power, or fame.

Group Therapy: See Chapter GENERAL TERMINOLOGY.

Hallucinations: A false sensory perception in the absence of an actual external stimulus. May be induced by emotional and other factors such as drugs, alcohol, and stress. May occur in any of the senses.

Hyperactive: See Chapter MENTAL RETARDATION.

Hyperkinetic: See Chapter MENTAL RETARDATION.

Hypnagogic: Related to the semiconscious state immediately preceding sleep; sometimes also loosely used as equivalent to "hypnotic state," "sleep-inducing," or "rim sleep."

Hypnosis: A state of increased receptivity to suggestion and direction, initially induced by the influence of another person.

Hysterical Neurosis: A neurosis characterized by a sudden psychogenic loss or disorder of function in response to an emotional stress. This disorder is divided into two subtypes:

1. **Conversion type:** An hysterical neurosis manifested by disorders of the special senses or the voluntary nervous system, such as blindness, deafness, anesthesia, paresthesia, paralysis, and impaired muscular coordination. A patient with this disorder may show indifference about his symptoms, which may actually provide secondary gains by winning him sympathy or relieving him of unpleasant responsibilities.

2. **Dissociative type:** An hysterical neurosis manifested by alterations in the patient's state of consciousness or in his identity, producing some symptoms as amnesia, somnambulism, fugue, or multiple personality.

Id: In Freudian theory, that part of the personality structure which harbors the unconscious instinctive desires and strivings of the individual.

Identification: A defense mechanism, operating unconsciously, by which an individual endeavors to pattern himself after another. Identification plays a major role in the development of one's personality and specifically of one's superego. To be differentiated from imitation, which is a conscious process.

Infantile Autism: See Chapter MENTAL RETARDATION.

Inferiority Complex: Feelings of inferiority stemming from real or imagined physical or social inadequ cies that may cause anxiety or other adverse reactions. The individual may overcompensate by excessive ambition or by the development of special skills, often in the very field in which he was originally handicapped.

Informed Consent: Agreement obtained from a subject, or from his authorized representative, to the subject's participation in an activity. The basic elements of informed consent are (1) a fair explanation of the procedures to be followed, including an identification of those which are experimental; (2) a description of the attendance discomforts and risks; (3) a description of the benefits to be expected; (4) a disclosure of appropriate alternative procedures that would be advantageous for the subject; (5) an offer to answer any inquiries concerning the procedures; (6) an instruction that the subject is free to withdraw his consent and to discontinue participation in the project or activity at any time.

Insanity: A vague, legal term for psychosis, now obsolete in psychiatric usage. Generally connotes: (1) a mental incompetence, (2) inability to distingiush "right from wrong," and/or (3) a condition that interferes with the individual's ability to care for himself or that constitutes a danger to himself or to others.

Instinct: An inborn drive. The primary human instincts include self-preservation and sexuality and for some proponents--aggression, the ego instincts, and "social" instincts. Freud also postulated a death instinct.

Intellectualization: The defense mechanism that utilizes reasoning as a defense against conscious confrontation with unconscious conflicts and their stressful emotions.

Intelligence Quotient (IQ): A numerical rating determined through psychological testing that indicates the approximate relationship of a person's mental age (MA) to his chronological age (CA). Expressed mathematically as $IQ = \dfrac{MA}{CA} \times 100$.

Thus, if MA=6 and CA=12, then IQ=6/12 x 100 or 50 (retarded). If MA=12 and CA=12, then IQ=100 (average). If MA=18 and CA=12, then IQ=150 (very superior). Since intellectual capacity is assumed to be fully developed about age 15, adult IQ's are computed by using a fixed arbitrary value of 1 for CA.

<u>Introjection</u>: A defense mechanism, operating unconsciously, whereby loved or hated external objects are taken within onself symbolically: The converse of projection. May serve as a defense against conscious recognition of intolerable hostile impulses. For example, in severe depression the individual may unconsciouly direct unacceptable hatred or aggression toward himself, i.e., toward the introjected object within himself. Related to the more primitive mechanism of incorporation.

<u>Latent Content</u>: The hidden (unconscious) meaning of thoughts or actions, especially in dreams or fantasies. In dreams it is expressed in distorted, disguised, condensed, and symbolic form, which is known as the manifest content.

<u>Magical Thinking</u>: A person's conviction that thinking equates with doing. Occurs in dreams, in children and primitive peoples, and in patients under a variety of conditions. Characterized by lack of realistic relationship between cause and effect.

<u>Maladaptive Model</u>: Belief that mental illness is a result of environmental pressures. The mental ill person should not be treated as diseased persons but rather individuals having severe problems of adjustment.

<u>Manic-Depressive Illness</u>: A major affective disorder characterized by severe mood swings and a tendency to remission and recurrence. It is divided into the following three subgroups:

1. <u>Depressed type</u>: A kind of manic-depressive illness consisting exclusively of depressive episodes characterized by severely depressed mood and by mental and motor retardation that may regress to stupor. Uneasiness, apprehension, perplexity, and agitation may also be present.

2. <u>Manic type</u>: A kind of manic-depressive illness consisting exclusively of manic episodes characterized by excessive elation, irritability, talkativeness, flight of ideas, and accelerated speech and motor activity.

3. <u>Manic-depressive type</u>: A vasculating combination of both manic and depressive behavior.

<u>Mental Illness</u>: A marked deviation from the norm in an individual's relations to others and severe disturbances in role performance.

<u>Mescaline</u>: An alkaloid originally derived from the peyote cactus, resembling amphetamine and adrenalin chemically; used experimentally to induce hallucination. Used by Indians of the Southwest in religious rites.

<u>Methadone</u>: A synthetic narcotic used to treat patients severaly addicted to heroin. In effect, it replaces one addiction with another less socially disabling addiction.

<u>Milieu Therapy</u>: The "therapeutic community" concept; the concept of the therapeutic or curative community may be described as an arrangement in which all of a patient's time in the hospital--not just the time he spends in therapy--is thought of as treatment. The milieu in which he finds himself, i.e., the hospital, is seen as exerting a powerful influence upon his emotional life and behavior. Every contact, every casual conversation with a fellow patient, a nurse, even a kitchen helper, is regarded as potentially therapeutic. It is an attempt to treat mental illness through a careful restructuring of the social environment. It implies a total team approach to treatment.

MMPI: See Chapter GENERAL TERMINOLOGY.

Moral Therapy: A humanitarian approach to dealing with the mentally ill prevalent
during the 19th Century. It emphasized kinder treatment of the patients, involving them in occupational and recreational training, as well as small group
encounters.

MSW: Master Degree Social Worker.

Narcissism (narcism): From Narcissus, figure in Greek mythology who feel in love
with his own reflected image. Self-love, as opposed to object-love (love of another). In psychoanalytic theory, cathexis (investment) of the psychic repre-
sentation of the self with libido (sexual interest and energy). Some degree of
narcissism is considered healthy and normal, but an excess interferes with
relations with others. To be distinguished from egotism, which carries the
connotation of self-centeredness, selfishness, and conceit. Egotism is but one
expression of narcissism.

Narcolepsy: Brief, uncontrollable episodes of sleeping.

Narcotic: Any drug, natural or synthetic, that produces sleep or even stupor and
relieves pain.

Negativism: Perverse opposition and resistance to suggestions or advice. Often observed in people who subjectively feel "pushed around." Seen normally in late
infancy. A common symptom in catatonic schizophrenia.

Neoplasm: A new growth or tumor. Neoplasms that affect behavior are primarily, but
not exclusively, found within the cranial cavity. Such neoplasms may cause
mental and behavioral disturbances in addition to neurological signs and
symptoms.

Nervous Breakdown: A nonmedical nonspecific term; a eusphenism for a mental disorder.

Neurosis: A functional nervous disorder without demonstrable physical lesion (or evident
of tissue damage), characterized chiefly by anxiety arising from some un-
resolved unconscious conflicts. This anxiety if either felt directly or controlled by various psychological mechanisms to produce other, subjectively
distressing symptoms. The neuroses are usually considered less severe than
the psychoses (although not always less disabling) because they manifest
neither gross personality disorganization nor gross distortion or misinterpre-
tation of external reality. The neuroses are classified according to the pre-
dominating symptoms. The common neuroses are:

1. Anxiety reaction: A neurosis characterized by anxious over-concern
occasionally progressing to panic; frequently associated with somatic
symptoms.

2. Depersonalization reaction: A neurosis characterized by feelings of un-
reality and of estrangement from the self, body, or surroundings. Different from the process of depersonalization, which may be a manifestation
of normal anxiety or of another mental disorder.

3. Depressive reaction: A neurosis manifested by an excessive reaction of depression due to an internal conflict or to an identifiable event, such as a loss of a loved person or a cherished possession.

4. Hypochondriacal reaction: A neurosis characterized by preoccupation with the body and with fear of presumed diseases of various organs. Although the fears are not delusional in quality, they persist despite reassurance.

5. Phobic reaction: Characterized by unreasonable, exaggerated fears and dreads about a specific object or situation (e.g., agoraphobia--fear of open spaces, claustrophobia--fear of closed places, acrophobia--fear of high places).

6. Obsessive-compulsive reaction: Characterized by repetition of thought or ritualistic act that occupies the mind and represses some thought from consciousness (e.g., bathing several times a day, extreme neatness, etc.).

7. Conversion reaction: (See alphabetical listing of this chapter).

8. Dissociative reaction: (See alphabetical listing of this chapter).

Non-directive Counseling: See Chapter GENERAL TERMINOLOGY.

Parapsychology: The study of metapsychic (psi) phenomena, i.e., events caused or perceived without the ordinary use of physical actions or senses (e.g., predicting outcome of throw of dice).

Passive-Dependent Personality: A disorder manifested by marked indecisiveness, emotional dependency, and lack of self-confidence. For diagnostic purposes, once considered to be a subtype of passive-aggressive personality.

Persona: A Jungian term for the personality "mask" or facade that each person presents to the outside world. Distinguished from the person's inner being or anima.

Personality: The characteristic way in which a person behaves; the deeply ingrained pattern of behavior that each person evolves, both consciously and unconsciously, as his style of life or way of being in adapting to his environment.

Personality Disorders: A group of mental disorders characterized by deeply ingrained maladaptive patterns of behavior, generally life-long in duration and consewuently often recognizable by the time of adolescence or earlier. Affecting primarily the personality of the individual, they are different in quality from neurosis and psychosis; defects in the personality.

1. Antisocial personality: A personality disorder characterized by a basic lack of socialization and by behavior patterns that bring the individual repeatedly into conflict with society. People with this disorder are incapable of significant loyalty to individuals, groups, or social values and are grossly selfish, callous, irresponsible, impulsive, and unable to feel guilt or to learn from experience and punishment. Frustration tolerance is low. Such individuals tend to blame others or offer plausible rationalizations for their behavior.

2. Asthenic personality: A personality disorder characterized by easy fatigability, low energy level, lack of enthusiasm, marked incapacity for enjoyment, and over-sensitivity to physical and emotional stress.

3. Compulsive personality: A personality disorder characterized by excessive rigidity, formality, and perfectionism. The individual expressed an exaggerated sense of duty and obedience, is stubborn in convictions, and extremely self-centered.

4. Cyclothymic personality (affective personality); A personality disorder characterized by recurring and alternating periods of depression and elation not readily attributable to external circumstances.

5. Explosive personality: A personality disorder characterized by gross outbursts of rage or of verbal or physical aggressiveness. Outbursts are strikingly different from the individual's usual behavior, and he may be regretful and repentant for them.

6. Hysterical personality (histrionic personality disorder): A personality disorder characterized by excitability, emotional instability, over-reactivity, and self-dramatization that is attention-seeking and often seductive, whether or not the individual is aware of its purpose. Often individuals with this disorder are immature, self-centered, vain, and unusually dependent on others.

7. Inadequate personality: A personality disorder characterized by ineffectual responses to emotional, social, intellectual, and physical demands. While the individual seems neither physically or mentally deficient, he does manifest inadaptability, ineptness, poor judgment, social instability, and lack of physical and emotional stamina.

8. Obsessive-compulsive personality (anankastic personality): A personality disorder characterized by excessive concern with conformity and adherence to standards of conscience. Individuals with this disorder may be rigid, over-inhibited, over-conscientious, over-dutiful, indecisive, perfectionistic, and unable to relax easily.

9. Paranoid personality: A personality disorder characterized by suspiciousness, over-sensitivity, jealousy, resentment, and hostility. The individual is extremely sensitive to criticism and often thinks that others dislike him and ridicule him. This provokes him to set goals far beyond his abilities and resulting failure deepens his sense of personal loss. He then becomes critical of others to ease his own injured self-esteem. He will blame his failure on others, and project on others his own hostile feelings.

10. Passive-aggressive personality: A personality disorder characterized by aggressive behavior manifested in various ways, such as obstructionism, pouting, procrastination, intentional inefficiency, or stubbornness. The three types of passive-aggressive personalities are:

   a) passive-dependent type: The individual shows his aggressive feelings to others by being passive, timid, dependent, unable to face responsibility or take action, or create controversy.

b) <u>passive-aggressive type</u>: The only way this individual can express his internal antagonism is through stubbornness, sullenness, procrastination and obstructiveness.

c) <u>aggressive type</u>: This individual is externally hostile by displaying a "chip-on-the-shoulder" attitude, constant belligerence, resentment and fight toward authority, and he can be openly destructive.

11. <u>Schizoid personality</u>: A personality disorder manifested by shyness, oversensitivity, seclusiveness, frequent day-dreaming, avoidance of close or competitive relationships, and often eccentricity. Individuals with this condition often react to the disturbing experiences and conflicts with apparent detachment and often unable to express hostility and ordinary aggressive feelings. This individual usually feels very lonely, isolated, and "wounded." He generally confided in no one and will resist the attempts of others to be friendly.

<u>Phenothiazine Derivatives</u>: A group of psychotropic drugs that, chemically, have in common the phenothiazine nucleus but that differ from one another through variations in chemical structure. As a group of drugs, the phenothiazines are also known as major tranquilizers possessing marked anti-anxiety and anti-psychotic properties.

<u>Projection</u>: A defense mechanism, operating unconsciously, whereby that which is emotionally unacceptable in the self is unconsciously rejected and attributed (projected) to others; placing blame for difficulties upon others.

<u>Projective Tests</u>: Psychological tests used as a diagnostic tool in which the test material is so unstructured that any response will reflect a projection some aspect of the subjects underlying personality and psychopathology. Among the most common projective tests are the Rorschach (inkblot) and the Thematic Apperception Test (TAT).

<u>Psychiatrist</u>: A physician (M.D.) specializing in mental, emotional, or behavioral disorders.

<u>Psychoanalysis</u>: Method of obtaining a detailed account of past and present mental and emotional experiences and repressions in order to determine the source and eliminate the pathologic mental or physical state produced by these mechanisms; largely the creation of Sigmund Freud. Includes a process of bringing to the conscious level repressed event: Utilizes two main methods--(1) dream analysis, and (2) free association.

<u>Psychodrama</u>: See Chapter GENERAL TERMINOLOGY.

<u>Psychogenic</u>: Of mental origin; concerning the development of the mind.

<u>Psychologist</u>: A specialist dealing mental, emotional, or behavioral disorders.

<u>Psychoneurotic Disorders</u>: Neuroses.

<u>Psychopharmacology</u>: The use of drugs to influence affective, emotional, and behavioral states or modify behavior.

1. <u>Stimulants</u>--used to stimulate cerebral activity producing wakefulness and a feeling of well-being (dextroamphetamine, benzedrine, and other amphetamines).

2. <u>Tranquilizers</u>--used to reduce various manic states, agitation, suspiciousness, uncooperativeness, and decrease delusions, disorientations, and hallucinations, i.e., chronic schizophrenia (thiothixene, thioridazine, and chlorpromazine).

3. <u>Anti-depressants</u>--used to reduce depression (amphetamines, tricyclic amines).

<u>Psychosis</u>: Characterized by severe personality disturbances which vary in duration and intensity. Psychotic episodes are irrational, prolonged, frequent, and unrealistic, whereas neurotic reactions may be mild and intermittent. The psychotic individual often replaced reality with his own fantasies or non-reality, whereas the neurotic individual realizes that something is wrong and does not replace reality with his own fantasies. The following are the major types of psychosis:

1. <u>Schizophrenia</u>: This is the most common type of psychosis, and is characterized by a shattered, disintegrated personality (not a "split" personality). The types of schizophrenia are:

   a. <u>Simple type</u>--characterized by marked indifference and a persistent continuous loss of interest, attention, concern, awareness, responsiveness, responsibility, and purpose. The personality seems to simply wither away. Social aberrations then become common, such as vagrancy, prostitution, and delinquency.

   b. <u>Hebephrenic type</u>--characterized by silly, incongruous and inappropriate laughter, hallucination, and fragments of delusional thoughts. Speech is disconnected, incoherent, and illogical. Personal habits of order often deteriorate, and bizarre mannerisms are present.

   c. <u>Catatonic type</u>--characterized by either the total lack of motion ("catatonic stupor") or by extreme motion ("catatonic excitement"-- extreme wild thrashing about).

   d. <u>Paranoid type</u>--characterized by delusions of persecution, hostile-aggressive behavior, and hallucinations of such things as outside powers, strange voices, rays, powerful forces, etc. Individuals may be very violent.

   e. <u>Childhood schizophrenia</u>--

      1) <u>Primary infantile autism</u>: characterized by existence in a state of isolation and separation; the child remains unresponsive to the mother. He appears to be living in a shell. There is a marked delay in communication skills, sometimes never learning to talk. The child is a slow learner in crawling and walking. He does not play with other children and prefers inanimate objects. He is

obsessed with circles, rocks a great deal, and is obsessed with the exact location of favorite things.

    2) <u>Symbiotic infantile psychosis</u>--opposite of autism. The child cannot be out of the mother's sight. He feels himself to be a part of the mother's body and never thinks of himself as being separate from his mother.

2. <u>Manic-Depressive</u> (different from schizophrenia where the personality disintegrates): The personality remains relatively well-organized with extreme disturbances of thought and emotions. Characterized by periods of extreme depression and then extreme mania (excitement, elation, agitation, hyperactivity). These changes may be frequent, inexplainable and inappropriate to environmental conditions. During the periods of depression the individual feels extremely hopeless and without purpose, during which time, he is suicidal.

3. <u>Depressive Reaction</u>: Characterized by deep prolonged spells of rejection, worthlessness, hopelessness, confusion, feelings of being evil and guilty, and extreme persecutory delusions. A break in a somewhat healthy personality as a result of stress on top of stress. Very often the individual will attempt suicide.

4. <u>Involutional Psychosis</u>: Extreme depression connected with middle age, when physical, mental, and emotional growth reach a peak and start to decline. It is related to the psychological stresses of middle age, such as loss of biological functions (childbearing, sexual potency), decline of sexual interest, and fear of insipid death. There are two types of involutional psychosis:

    a. <u>Involutional depressive reaction</u> (involutional melancholia)--an active depression during the middle ages that is characterized by weeping, moaning, intense feelings of guilt, uselessness, sorry over injury to others, and a feeling of the need to be punished.

    b. <u>Involutional paranoid reaction</u>--middle-aged fearfulness, agitation, tenseness, but not depression. Characterized by evil thoughts of others and persecutory ideas.

5. <u>Psychosis of Old Age</u>: Related to organic changes in old age.

    a. <u>Psychosis with cerebral arteriosclerosis</u>--"atherosclerosis" or narrowing of the arterial tube of deposits building up (not hardening of the arteries). Characterized by confusion, agitiation, restlessness, lessening of mental and physical capacity, incoherence, emotional instability, impairment of memory, bewilderment, irritability, depression, anxiety, quarrelsomeness, violent outbursts, feelings of persecution, and neglectfulness of personal appearances.

    b. <u>Senile psychosis</u>--general "wearing out" of neurological and glandular systems. Characterized by marked deterioration of mental and emotional facilities, memory failure, ideas become meager, expressions is elementary; individual is confused about time and place and people are wrongly identified; the individual becomes stingy, gets lost, his judgment about danger fails, he becomes quarrelsome and suspicions.

6.   Paranoia: The obvious symptom is extreme feelings of persecution. The individual otherwise has a well-integrated personality. He simply has a totally unrealistic delusional system concerning persecution.

Psychomatic: Interrelationship between the mind and body; a pathological condition due to emotional or psychogenic factors.

Psychotherapy: See Chapter GENERAL TERMINOLOGY.

Rapport: In psychiatry, the conscious feeling of harmonious accord, mutual responsiveness, and sympathy that contributes to the patient's confidence in the therapist and willineness to work cooperatively with him. To be distinguished from transference, which is unconscious.

Rationalization: Attempting to prove that one's behavior is justified and thus worthy of self and social approval.

Reaction Formation: A defense mechanism, operating unconsciously, wherein attitudes and behavior are adopted that are the opposites of impulses the individual harbors either consciously or unconsciously (e.g., excessive moral zeal may be a reaction to strong but repressed anti-social impulses); preventing dangerous desires from being expressed by exaggerating opposed attitudes and using them as barriers.

Reality Therapy: See Chapter GENERAL TERMINOLOGY.

Reflective Listening: See Chapter GENERAL TERMINOLOGY.

Regression: The partial or symbolic return to more infantile patterns of reacting.

Repression: A defense mechanism, operating unconsciously, that banishes unacceptable ideas, affects, or impulses, from consciousness or that keeps out of consciousness what has never been conscious. Although not subject to voluntary recall, the repressed material may emerge in disguised form. Preventing painful thoughts from entering consciousness.

Rigidity: In psychiatry, refers to an individual's excessive resistance to change.

Rogerian Therapy: See Chapter GENERAL TERMINOLOGY.

Shock Treatment: A form of psychiatric treatment in which electric current, insulin, carbon dioxide, or Indoklon is administered to the patient and results in a loss of consciousness or a convulsive or comatose reaction to alter favorably the course of the illness. Some common types of shock therapy are:

1.   Carbon dioxide therapy: A form of inhalation treatment in which carbon dioxide gas is administered to the point of unconsciousness in order to cause emotional abreactions and alleviation of anxiety.

2.   Electroconvulsive treatment (ECT): Use of electric current to induce unconsciousness and/or convulsive seizures. Most effective in the treatment of depression. Introduced by Cerletti and Bini in 1938. Modifications are electronaccosis, producing sleep-like states, and electro-stimulation, which avoids convulsions.

3. Indoklon therapy: A form of shock treatment in which a convulsive seizure is produced by intravenous injection or inhalation of the drug, Indoklon.

4. Insulin coma therapy (ICT): A treatment primarily for schizophrenia in which insulin is injected in large enough doses to produce profound hypoglycemia (low blood sugar) resulting in coma. First used by Manfred Sakel in 1933. Its use in the United States has decreased since the introduction of tranquilizers.

Subconscious: Obsolescent term in psychiatry. Formerly used to include the preconscious (what can be recalled without effort) and the unconscious.

Sublimation: A defense mechanism, operating unconsciously, by which instinctual drives, consciously unacceptable, are diverted into personally and socially acceptable channels; working off frustrated sexual desires in non-sexual activities.

Superego: In psychoanalytic theory, that part of the personality associated with ethics, standards, and self-criticism. It is formed by the infant's identification with important and esteemed persons in his early life, particularly parents. The supposed or actual wishes of these significant persons are taken over as part of the child's own personal standards to help form the "conscience". In late life they may become anachronistic and self-punitive, especially in neurotic persons.

Suppression: The conscious effort to control and conceal unacceptable impulses, thoughts, feelings, or acts.

Symbiosis: In psychiatry, denotes a mutually-reinforcing relationship between two disturbed persons who are dependent on each other.

T-Groups: See Chapter GENERAL TERMINOLOGY.

Therapeutic Community: (See Milieu Therapy).

Transactional Analysis (TA): See Chapter GENERAL TERMINOLOGY.

Transient Situational Disturbance: A more or less transient disorder of any severity (including psychosis) that represents an acute reaction to overwhelming stres such as the severe crying spells, loss of appetite, and social withdrawal of a child separated from its mother; or, in an adult, a reaction to an unwanted pregnancy manifested by suicidal gestures and hostile complaints. The symptoms generally recede as the stress diminishes.

Tranquilizer: A drug that decreases anxiety and agitation, usually without causing drowsiness. Divided into two groups:

1. Major tranquilizers: Drugs such as phenothiazines which produce relief from symptoms of psychosis.

2. Minor tranquilizers: Drugs that are used predominantly to diminish neurotic anxiety.

Weed System: See Chapter GENERAL TERMINOLOGY.

Wernicke's Syndrome: See Chapter GENERAL MEDICAL TERMINOLOGY.

Chapter VIII
SYMBOLS USED IN RECORD KEEPING AND CHARTING

Very often activity therapists are required to read the charts and progress notes on their clients in order to program meaningful, therapeutic activities. Unless one is familiar with the language used in charting, he or she may well be at a loss to interpret the information in the clients' records.

The approach taken in this chapter is to simply give the individual some of the most basic symbols used in charting. Each facility may have several symbols unqiue to their own needs. However, the following language is generally accepted in treatment settings and should be a great value to students or new activity therapy employees.

Symbol	Meaning
$\bar{a}$	before
$\bar{p}$	after
$\bar{c}$	with
$\bar{s}$	without
$\bar{q}$	every
$\bar{o}$	other
d	day
q.o.d.	every other day
$\overline{xc}$	except
noc	night
b.i.d.	twice a day
t.i.d.	three times a day
q.i.d.	four times a day
h.s.	hour of sleep
a.c.	before meals
p.c.	after meals
BM	bowel movement
B & B	bowel and bladder
BMR	basal metabolic rate
BP	blood pressure

Symbol	Meaning
CNS	central nervous system
D & C	dilatation and curettage
D.T.'s	delirium tremens
D & V	diarrhea and vomiting
ECG/EKG	electrocardiogram
E.C.T.	electroconvulsive therapy
E.S.T.	electroshock therapy
E.E.G.	electroencephalogram
Hb	hemoglobin
HT	hypertension
I.V.	intravenous (into the vein)
I.M.	intramuscular (into the muscle)
n	normal
O.R.	operating room
PRN/p.r.n.	given as needed
Rx	prescription/treatment
S.O.B.	shortness of breath
T & A	tonsil and adenoids
TB	tuberculin
V.D.	venereal disease
V.D.G.	gonorrhea
cap	capsule
tab	tablet
Sig.	instructions (when to take drugs)
$\overline{aa}$	of each
NPO	nothing by mouth
BJM	bones, joints, muscles

Symbol	Meaning
NP	neuropsychiatric
G.I.	gastrointestinal
C.V.R.	cardio-vascular-respiration
G.U.	genitourinary
M.L.	midline
N.S.R.	normal sinus rhythm
Tach	tachycardia
LKS	liver, kidney, spleen
♂	male
♀	female
C.N.	cranial nerves
D.T.R.	deep tendon reflexes
P.N.D.	post nasal drip
fx	fracture
pt.	patient
ad. lib.	as patient can tolerate
up ad. lib.	allow patient to move around as much as he feels he can
state	immediately
BRP	bathroom privileges
Ca	cancer
I.U.D.	intrauterine device
cath.	catheterize
post op	after surgery
pre op	before surgery; also means pre op medication
prep	prepare for surgery
C.P.	cerebral palsied

Symbol	Meaning
M.S.	multiple sclerosis
M.D.	muscular dystrophy
RT/TR	Recreation Therapist/Therapeutic Recreation
√TRS	Therapeutic Recreation Specialist
MTRS	Master Therapeutic Recreation Specialist
P.T.	physical therapy
O.T.	occupational therapy
O.T.R.	Registered Occupational Therapist
R.N.	Registered Nurse
L.P.N.	Licensed Practicel Nurse
TMR/TMH	trainable mentally retarded or handicapped
EMR/EMH	educable mentally retarded or handicapped
L.D.	learning disability
D.D.	developmental disability
R.T.	Recreation Therapist
w/c	wheelchair
DOA	dead on arrival
O.D.	overdose
AMA	against medical advice
C-5	cervical lesion at the fifth vertebra
T-5	thoracic lesion at the fifth vertebra
L-5	lumbar lesion at the fifth vertebra
R.O.M.	range of motion
NWB	no weight-bearing (as in crutch walking)
PWB	partial weight-bearing
FWB	full weight-bearing
OBS	organic brain syndrone

Symbol	Meaning
CVA	cerebral vascular accident - stroke
FUO	fever of unknown origin

REFERENCES

_____, A Review of Mental Illness. New York: J. B. Roerig Division, Chas. Pfizer & Co., Inc., 1968.

American Association for Health, Physical Education, and Recreation Committee on Adapted Physical Education. "Guiding Principles for Adapted Physical Education." Journal of the American Association for Health, Physical Education, and Recreation. 23:4:15, April, 1952, p. 15.

Arey, L. B. (ed.). Dorland's Illustrated Medical Dictionary. Philadelphia: W. B. Saunders and Company, 1957.

Avedon, Elliott M. Therapeutic Recreation Service. Englewood Cliffs, New Jersey: Prentice-Hall, 1974.

Baumeister, A. A. (ed.). Mental Retardation. Chicago: Aldine Publishing Company, 1971.

Berne, E. Games People Play. New York: Grove Press, 1964.

Berne, E. A Layman's Guide to Psychiatry and Psychoanalysis. New York: Grove Press, Inc., 1947.

Berne, E. Transactional Analysis in Psychotherapy. New York: Grove Press, 1961.

Bry, A., Inside Psychotherapy. New York: Signet, 1972.

Chapman, F. M. Recreation Activities for the Handicapped. New York: Ronald Pr ss Company.

Connor, F. P. and Cohen, M. (eds.). Leadership Preparation. Report of a Special Study Institute, Tappan Zee Inn, Nyack, New York. March 28-31, 1973. Funded by U. S. Office of Education under Public Law 91-230 as amended (OEG-0-72-4121) (603).

Davis, P. Medical Terminology in Hospital Practice. London: Heinemann, 1969.

English, H. B. and English, A. C. A Comprehensive Dictionary of Psychological and Psychoanalytical Terms. New York: Longmans, Green and Company, 1958.

English. O. S. and Finch, S. M. Introduction to Psychiatry. New York: W. W. Norton and Company, Inc., 1957.

Fagan, J. and Sh herd, I. (eds.). Gestalt Therapy Now: Theory, Techniques, Applications. New York: Harper and Row, 1970.

Fagan, J. and Shepherd, I. (eds.). What is Gestalt Therapy? New York: Perennial Library, 1970.

Fairchild, H. P. Dictionary of Sociology and Related Sciences. Ames, Iowa: Littlefield, Adams, and Company, 1959.

Frye, V. and Peters, M. Therapeutic Recreation: Its Theory, Philosophy, and Practice. Harrisburg, Pennsylvania: Stackpole, 1972.

Glasser, W. Reality Therapy: A New Approach to Psychiatry. New York: Harper and Row, 1965.

Good, C. V. (ed.). Dictionary of Education. New York: McGraw-Hill Company, 1945.

Grossman, H. J. Manual on Terminology and Classification in Mental Retardation. Baltimore: Garamond/Pridemark Press, 1973.

Harper, R. A. Psychoanalysis and Psychotherapy. Englewood Cliffs, New Jersey: Prentice-Hall, Inc., 1959.

Hoerr, N. L. and Osol, Arthur (eds.). Blakiston's New Gould Medical Dictionary. New York: McGraw-Hill Company, The Blakiston Division, 1956.

Hunt, V. V. Recreation for the Handicapped. New York: Prentice-Hall, Inc., 1955.

James, M. and Jongeward, D. Born to Win: Transactional Analysis with Gestalt Experiments. Reading, Massachusetts: Addison-Wesley Publishing Company, 1971.

Knowles, M. and Knowles, H. Introduction to Group Dynamics. New York: Association Press, 1959.

Kraus, R. Therapeutic Recreation Service: Principles and Practices. Philadelphia: W. B. Saunders, 1973.

MacEachern, M. T. Hospital Organization and Management. Chicago: Physician's Record Company, 1957.

MacLachlan, J. M., "Cultural Factors in Health and Disease," Patients, Physicians and Illness. Glencoe, Illinois: The Free Press, 1958.

Meyer, H. D. and Brightbill, C. K. Recreation Administration. New Jersey: Prentice-Hall, Inc., 1956.

_____, "Orientation Manual, Physical Medicine, and Rehabilitation." Washington, D. C.: Veterans Administration Department of Medicine and Surgery, March, 1966, p. 183.

Parsons, T., "Definitions of Health and Illness in the Light of American Values and Social Structure," Patients, Physicians and Illness. Glencoe, Illinois: The Free Press, 1958, p. 32.

Perls, F. S. Gestalt Therapy Verbatim. Lafayette, California: Real People Press, 1969.

Perls, F., Hefferline, R. F. and Goodman, P. Gestalt Therapy: Excitement and Growth in the Human Personality. New York: Delta, 1951.

Price, A. L. The American Nurse's Dictionary. Philadelphia: W. B. Saunders Company, 1949.

Sessoms, H. D. (ed.). Glossary of Recreation and Park Terms: Bulletin No. 95. Arlington, Virginia: National Recreation and Park Association, Inc., 1972.

Stein, J. U., "Adapted Physical Education," Journal of Health, Physical Education and Recreation. 40:5:45; May, 1969, p. 46.

Stein, T. A. and Sessoms, D. Recreation and Special Populations. Boston: Holbrook Press, Inc., 1973.

Taber, C. W. Taber's Cyclopedic Medical Dictionary. Philadelphia: F. A. Davis Company, 1962.

Taylor, N. B. (ed.). Stedman's Medical Dictionary. Baltimore: The Williams and Wilkins Company.

Timmins, L. Understanding Through Communication: Structured Experiments in Self-Exploration. Springfield, Illinois: Charles C. Thomas, 1972.

Tourney, G., "Treatment in the Modern Mental Hospital." Albany, New York: New York Department of Mental Hygiene, 1966.

Scarf, M., "In the Therapeutic Community Patients Are Doctors," Time. New York, May 25, 1969, p. 109.

_____. Training Manual for a Rehabilitation Program in a Nursing Home or Extended Care Facility. Springfield, Illinois: Department of Public Health, 1973.

Tupper, F. E., "Hospital Recreation Today: Some Basic Concepts," The American Recreation Journal, November, 1960.

Valett, R. E. Modifying Children's Behavior. Belmont, California: Fearson Publishers, 1969.

Warren, H. C. Dictionary of Psychology. Boston: Houghton-Mifflin Company, 1934.

_____. Webster's Seventh New Collegiate Dictionary. Springfield, Massachusetts: G. and C. Merriam Company, 1965.

Willard. H. S. and Spackman, C. S. Principles of Occupational Therapy. Philadelphia: J. B. Lippincott, 1954.

Young, C. and Barger, J. Learning Medical Terminology Step by Step. St. Louis: Mosby, 1967.

ADDITIONAL TERMS